# ROAR

How to Build a Resilient Organization
the World-Famous San Diego Zoo Way

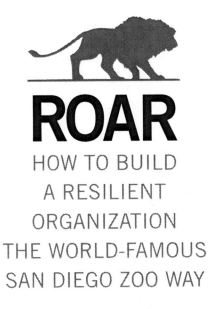

# ROAR

HOW TO BUILD
A RESILIENT
ORGANIZATION
THE WORLD-FAMOUS
SAN DIEGO ZOO WAY

SAN DIEGO ZOO
GLOBAL

Sandy Asch and Tim Mulligan

HIGHPOINT
EXECUTIVE
PUBLISHING

This edition published by Highpoint Executive Publishing. For information, write to info@highpointpubs.com.

First Edition

ISBN: 978-0-9861585-8-2

Library of Congress Cataloging-in-Publication Data

Asch, Sandy
Mulligan, Tim
*Roar: How to Build a Resilient Organization the World-Famous San Diego Zoo Way*
Includes index.

Summary: "In today's volatile times, every organization looking to prosper needs resilience—the ability of employees to quickly adapt to disruptions while continually enhancing performance and brand equity. This groundbreaking book shows you how the San Diego Zoo has created that resilience with a roar of purpose and passion that drives engagement and inspires extraordinary effort."
– Provided by publisher.

ISBN: 978-0-9861585-8-2 (hardbound)
1.Business 2. Leadership

Library of Congress Control Number: 2016935724

Design: Sarah Clarehart
Cover concept and logo: Kambiz Mehrafshani

Manufactured in the United States of America

10  9  8  7  6  5  4  3  2  1

# ROAR Endorsements

"*ROAR* is a must-read for any organization looking to build competitive advantage through its people. The iconic, world-class San Diego Zoo shares a compelling lesson in cultural transformation, alignment, and engagement to build a rich legacy of resilience. We're honored to have played a part through our decade-long partnership, and applaud Sandy and Tim for sharing this wonderful journey."

— Les Rechan, CEO, Halogen Software

"Sandy Asch has collaborated with Tim Mulligan to capture the essence of what it takes to build a winning culture. By utilizing the concepts in *ROAR*, one can successfully lead in the ever-changing business climate that the world demands today. A refreshing approach from an inspirational leader in her own right!"

— Kevin Friar, EVP NALCO Champion-Ecolab

"Sandy Asch and Tim Mulligan collaborate masterfully in illustrating how the key elements of a resilient culture are attainable to any organization choosing to embrace this transformative mindset."

— Denise Hujing, Senior Vice President,
BB&T-John Burnham Insurance Services

"As a veteran HR practitioner, it's encouraging to see the attention *ROAR* brings to the topic of organizational resilience. I have experienced firsthand how an organization and its workforce can be more than just sustainable, but even thrive when a resilient culture is established. *ROAR* is a fun, enjoyable, and worthwhile read, with compelling examples and useful takeaways that companies can integrate into their human capital function."

**– Sallie Larsen, Managing Director and
Chief Human Capital Officer, LPL Financial**

"In *ROAR* authors Sandy Asch and Tim Mulligan have flung the gates open to the world-famous San Diego Zoo organization and culture. They artfully integrate organizational and individual employee resilience to tell an energetic story with concepts that are freshly redrawn."

**– Judith Enns, Ph.D, Executive Vice President,
HR Division, Eastridge Workforce Solutions**

"Being overwhelmed is contagious and often falsely energizing! When life experiences reinforce reacting and even celebrating overcoming overwhelm. *ROAR* gives real world, organizational and personal examples that drive a mindset shift to adapt, to rebalance, renew and align versus react. A wonderful read that makes you think and choose!"

**– Melissa Master-Holder, Vice President
Learning and Development, LPL Financial**

# Contents

# Foreword

In 2016, the world-famous San Diego Zoo reached a milestone that few organizations anywhere have matched—100 years in existence! We decided to recognize this achievement with a year-long centennial celebration. Its theme is "The ROAR Heard 'Round the World"—referencing our origin, when a lone lion left in a cage in Balboa Park after the 1915-1916 Panama-California Exposition was heard roaring in the distance by local San Diego physician, Dr. Harry Wegeforth.

Upon hearing this momentous roar, Dr. Harry turned to his brother and said, "Wouldn't it be splendid if San Diego had a zoo?" And the rest is history. A 100-year revolution was born. That one "splendid," singular roar evolved into the "Roar Heard 'Round the World," transforming a single parcel of land into one of our planet's most beloved and inspiring destinations.

Indeed, there's no place quite like the world-famous San Diego Zoo, which today has grown into San Diego Zoo Global, operating the San Diego Zoo, the San Diego Zoo Safari Park, and the San Diego Zoo Institute for Conservation Research. We not only delight and educate 5 million guests annually through our innovative, expansive exhibits and habitats, but also are known as a leading global research organization, and a world leader at connecting people to wildlife and conservation, with more than 140 field projects in 80 countries that have saved many species from extinction.

How have we achieved this world-famous success? We have learned how to win the hearts and minds of our employees to evoke a ROAR of purpose and passion, while creating a team of world-famous leaders. That's why the Zoo is not only known as a sanctuary for animals, but also a sanctuary for employees who love their jobs and accomplish extraordinary things. We call that resilience, which is the topic of this book.

*Roar: How to Build Organizational Resilience the World-Famous San Diego Zoo Way* shows you how to unleash the full potential of your most valuable asset, your employees, to create lasting organizational resiliency rivaling that of our world-famous San Diego Zoo. Authors Tim Mulligan and Sandy Asch have been instrumental in driving our program in recent years. In 2004, Tim came onboard as chief human resources officer, full of innovative ideas that he had put to work with previous employers. He soon met Sandy, the principal at Alliance for Organizational Excellence LLC, a global consulting company. A powerful synergy was engaged as the two went to work on rolling out a wave of exceptional branded programs that have further expanded our world-famous reputation to the areas of leadership, employee engagement, and resilience. This book tells the story.

We have found that when you are able to rally people around a cause they care about deeply, extraordinary things are possible. And that's how our 100-year-old nonprofit organization continues to live up to its reputation as "world famous." I encourage you to read this book and achieve your own version of our world-famous resilience. You'll learn to master winds of change, overcome stress and adversity, thrive in times of chaos, remain constant in pursuit of your vision, and accomplish extraordinary things.

**Doug Myers, President and CEO, San Diego Zoo Global**

# Acknowledgments

Gratitude to Doug Myers and San Diego Zoo Global leaders Ted Molter, Beth Branning, David Page, Adam Ringler, Bob Wiese, Dwight Scott, Becky Lynn, and Allison Alberts, Ph.D., for their insights and ideas. Thanks also to Steisha Ponczoch for coordinating myriad details, always with a smile; the SDZG Human Resources team, for their support and making the Rules of Engagement stick; Sheryl Roush for her extraordinary leadership training; as well as Michael Roney and the Highpoint Executive Publishing team for believing in this book, holding our hands every step of the way, and synthesizing our ideas into a work that exceeded our expectations.

## Sandy

Thanks to all the participants in Excellence at Work over the past 18 years for creating new possibilities and teaching me what excellence really means. I am still learning. Also to Eric Marin for keeping me grounded in the vision, reminding me who I want to be, and aligning with my dream; Santi Darmodjo and Sonny Brandtner for bringing credibility to the Resilience at Work Calculator; Luisa Cicero for partnering with me with love, passion, and enthusiasm; Melissa Master-Holder for her humility, grace, and support whenever I needed help; David Winkelman for his creative brilliance and partnership in all wild ideas; Eric Carlson for making the connection between resilience and finance; John Schierer for his wisdom; Tim Mulligan, for supporting my wild ideas and making things happen behind the scenes; and Daniel Naor for his unconditional stand for the possibility of a world filled with compassion and generosity. Most importantly, I am thankful for my son, Adam Sloane. I am honored to be your mother. You inspire me to keep growing and help me to remember what's really important. ROAR!

## Tim

I would like to acknowledge the amazing HR team I work with day in and day out for always GOING FOR THE ROAR! And for those who have helped me along the way, thank you, thank you, thank you: Michelle and the marketing team; Doug, for letting me run with this; Debra, for being a confidante and sounding board; Berit Durler, for getting me into the zoo world; and, of course, Sean.

# Introduction

*More than education, more than experience, more than training, a person's level of resilience will determine who succeeds and who fails. That's true in the cancer ward, it's true in the Olympics, and it's true in the boardroom."*

– Dean Becker

The way we're working isn't working. The manic demand and pressures of the workplace have caused us to neglect our health and wellbeing, our families, and our personal lives. We are sicker, more disconnected, and less fulfilled. There is little buffer between demand and response, call for action and expected result, messages requesting information and anticipated acknowledgment. We're struggling to maintain peace, calm, and tranquility in the storm of stress, and the focus and energy we need to harness innovation and creativity.

It's no wonder there is so much illness and despair in the world. It has been estimated that 75 to 90 percent of all visits to primary care physicians are for stress-related problems. We are being challenged to adopt a new normal—a new way of thinking about how we work—to find a better way to balance the pressures and demands of work with a healthy personal life, and rediscover joy, equanimity, and peace that extend beyond our workday into our homes and communities, and ultimately the world.

## Building Immunity to Disruption

It's a fact that we're living in disruptive times. Industries are collapsing, financial markets are imploding, oil and commodity prices are plummeting, and terrorism is shutting down major urban areas. Preventing these hardships would be everyone's first choice. But in an increasingly complex and volatile world, it's impossible.

To survive and thrive, organizations must be purposeful, agile, tenacious, and balanced. They must find a sustainable means to proactively, protect their most valued assets and resources—their employees—to mitigate the risk of economic pressures and uncertainty and continue to innovate and thrive. "Today it's become essential for companies (and individuals) to become more agile—not just in the face of the risks we know, but in the face of the ones we won't see coming," says Andrew Zolli, the executive director and curator of PopTech and the co-author (with Ann Marie Healy) of *Resilience: Why Things Bounce Back*.

The key to not only surviving the events of today's world but prospering is resilience. While human resilience may be thought of as a personality trait, in the aggregate, groups, organizations, and even communities can learn to develop a "culture of resilience," which manifests itself as a form of "psychological immunity" to, or the ability to rebound from, the untoward effects of adversity.

Resilience is more than survival. It is the ability of the individual and the organization to endure while remaining true to closely held values. Resilient people and companies not only rebound from challenging circumstances, they seek out meaningful ways to learn from those experiences and build capacity for the future.

## Resilience Means Growing Stronger

Resilience is a hot topic in business. Some might say it's the new buzzword, especially as it relates to financial resilience. Does it matter in the workplace? Yes, probably more than intelligence, skill, or ambition. Resilience is the backbone of any organization—the ability of its employees to respond effectively to the demands and pressures of the work world to meet goals and expectations while possessing perpetual fulfillment. The business world has excelled at mastering the art of achievement, yet many still hunger for fulfillment. The lack of fulfillment in the workplace may indeed be the reason so many organizations constantly struggle with recruitment and retention, and—as

Gallup has proven for the past decade or more—why they have been beleaguered by concerns about declining employee engagement.

The solution to happiness and wellbeing is to cultivate resilience. Resilience is complex, subject to varied interpretations. It is perhaps one of the greatest puzzles of human nature. Resilient people possess five key characteristics: the ability to control their response; proficiency at managing time and energy; deftness at consistent authenticity; finesse at maintaining meaningful connectedness; and a prevailing perseverance.

Resilience is something you typically realize you have after the fact, perhaps following a challenging experience. Yet it is most valuable when developed before the fact. You tend to underestimate its importance when things are going well, and you most sorely feel its absence when times are tough. Everyone needs resilience. It's a virtue essential to growth and key to happiness and success.

The Biosphere 2 project was created as a research tool for scientists to study Earth's living systems, and it allowed scientists to experiment with farming and innovation in a way that didn't harm the planet. One of the most significant discoveries made by the scientists had to do with the wind's role in a tree's life. It was found that the trees inside Biosphere 2 grew rapidly—more rapidly than they did outside of the dome—but they also fell over before reaching maturation.

After studying the root systems and outer layers of bark, the scientists realized that a lack of wind actually caused a deficiency of stress wood. Stress wood helps a tree position itself for optimal sun absorption, and it also helps trees grow more solid. Without stress wood, a tree can grow quickly, but it cannot support itself fully. It cannot withstand normal wear and tear, and survive. In other words, the trees needed some stress in order to thrive in the long run.

While many people would prefer to avoid stress in the workplace, we all know it's inevitable. Rather than viewing stress as a negative factor, it can be used to build resilience; and enable employees to thrive by developing critical skills and characteristics to support themselves— to move through the demands of the business world with greater ease.

## Building a Resilient Workforce at San Diego Zoo Global

Since a strong sense of purpose is a vital component of resilience, it follows that the most successful organizations and people possess clearly articulated value systems and a vision and mission that engage both hearts and minds. This is the case at San Diego Zoo Global. "What has saved San Diego Zoo Global and allowed us to prosper for the past 100 years, becoming one of, if not *the* most recognized zoos in the world, is our purpose," says Doug Myers, SDZG president and CEO. "Everyone who works for us, volunteers, or supports us shares a common set of values. Although SDZG's mission and strategy have changed, the values have always remained constant."

Anyone can lead, but few are able to win the hearts and minds of their team to evoke a roar of purpose and passion. When you rally people around a cause they care about deeply, your organization can succeed at a level beyond any previous accomplishments. In fact, many such milestones have occurred while SDZG has grown steadily over the decades.

More than 5 million guests visit the San Diego Zoo and San Diego Zoo Safari Park each year to view the renowned animal exhibits, enjoy the attractions, and learn about conservation. SDZG is not only known as a sanctuary for animals, but also a sanctuary for people. "We must take extra good care of our employees, as we do our animals, to ensure we are able to achieve our goals and fulfill our mission," says Myers. "Although we pay our employees fairly, we realize they deserve much more. This is why we go the extra mile to take care of them and support them in living a healthy, balanced life."

Building a resilient workforce at SDZG is founded on the purposeful architecture of an organizational culture that thrives on the mission and purpose. Leaders are grounded in doing the right things, and are called forward by an overwhelming passion for the mission. Commitment to the vision of ending extinction is infectious.

Becky Lynn was hired in 1975 and currently serves as director of employee communications. Forty years later, she is still as excited about her job as when she first started working for the Zoo. "I stay because of the important conservation and animal care work we do, as well as the amazing people I've been fortunate to work with," Lynn explains. "In the early 1980s, SDZG and other conservation organizations brought in the last 22 California condors from the wild to help them back from the brink of extinction. It was a controversial move at the time. Our people were so dedicated to this challenge. We were excited together at each success. My job has been to communicate these and other conservation achievements for all employees to share.

"There are now more than 400 California condors, with over half of them returned to the wild," Lynn adds. "Recently, my 37-year-old son was hiking in the mountains above Big Sur and he had the opportunity to sit quietly near two wild California condors on a ledge. He was thrilled, and so was I. It felt as if my career and connection with SDZG had come full circle. We work to conserve these endangered species so that our children and grandchildren will be able to appreciate them in their natural habitat—and that is exactly what happened. A week later, my son took his 8-year-old daughter camping on the beach in Big Sur and they saw two California condors flying above. Heartwarming!"

## Going for the ROAR

It seems everyone wants to work at the Zoo. After all, how many people have the opportunity to feed breakfast to lions or watch monkeys during their lunch break? SDZG's recruitment tag line "Put Your Passion for Wildlife to Work!" attracts approximately 15,000 applications each year from highly talented people eager to be part of its "world-famous" organization. Of these, about 900 are accepted. Once they are hired, people don't want to leave: the average tenure of Zoo employees is 20-plus years, with an attrition rate of less than 5 percent.

Above all, the factor that bonds SDZG employees, volunteers, and supporters is their commitment to the ROAR. The ROAR is the list of values or core tenets of the San Diego Zoo Global culture. "We like to say those are the things that have always been here," says Ted

Molter, chief marketing officer. "They always will be here. They're not necessarily things we're good at. They are the things that we care about and we've always cared about since the Zoo was founded in the 1900s; the things we will continue to care about far into the future."

Now, 100 years later, "the ROAR" is the theme of SDZG's centennial. The "ROAR heard 'round the world" is set to include an event where thousands of supporters gather to create a ROAR, attempting a record for the Guinness World Records. "The ROAR symbolizes the impact we have in the world." says Myers. This includes more than 140 field projects in 80 countries; the drive to save endangered species; renowned education programs that have touched hundreds of thousands of children; and the effect SDZG has had on millions of people from around the world who have visited the parks.

## Becoming World Famous

Conventional thinking used to be that SDZG's reputation would ensure its long-term success. But, the organization also realized that in order to accomplish this goal, it would have to nurture world-famous leaders.

Just as the Zoo has been recognized internationally as a leader in conservation, working tirelessly to save endangered species from extinction, it has also been acclaimed for its efforts to build a "world-famous" place to work. It has flaws like any other organization, but is fiercely committed to building a culture where every person is fully engaged in providing a GRRREAT guest experience. After all, if you have the reputation as a world-famous organization, it's important to be a world-class employer too. To accomplish this, SDZG has embarked on a systematic Zoo Print for Success—a road map to develop best-in-class people practices, all on a shoestring budget. If SDZG can, you can!

As with any new employee, interns attend extensive training, job shadow animal experts, and are rigorously oriented to the "world-famous" way. On day one, new hires are imprinted for success with the Rules of Engagement. Described in Chapter 2, these are SDZG's code of conduct, a set of standards and expectations. The rules establish a common language, shared vision, and accountability for being world famous. They help to build a positive, productive workplace and a resilient culture.

And, thus begins the story—how SDZG is forging a leadership identity, and building an organization that keeps getting better and better. Its success over the years has been validated by significant growth in the number of visitors to the Zoo and Safari Park, with park attendance in 2014 breaking a 100-year record. It has achieved a 10 percent improvement in overall employee engagement scores, and has received seven awards for workplace excellence. Its bold, audacious goal is to end extinction. It isn't the perfect organization, but we think it's doing a GRRREAT job.

In *Roar: How to Build a Resilient Organization the World-Famous San Diego Zoo Way*, we share with you what SDZG did to get where it is, and how they did it. We offer you a Zoo Print for Success—a roadmap peppered with creative ideas and insider stories to build resilient employees who are proud and passionate. The book begins with an exploration of resilience, including the five-step Resilience at Work™ model, and how to calculate the financial impact of resilience. Then you will learn about many of the innovative strategies SDZG uses to build a resilient organization. Next, in each of the sections, you will delve into the five core competencies of resilience supported by real stories from the San Diego Zoo.

We will show you how to build a resilient organization while having fun, even if you don't have a monkey exhibit. So put on your safari hat and come along for the ride.

## PART ONE:

# Learning to Roar

Organizational resilience means success. Achieving resilience for your organization means reclaiming self-control, realigning conditions, reimagining communications, renewing connections, and rebalancing commitment. The world-famous San Diego Zoo, operated by San Diego Zoo Global (SDZG), has followed those principles, creating a world-class workforce through a sustained high-performance culture, organizational goals and drivers, a big-picture plan for the future, and numerous employee engagement programs.

CHAPTER

# 1

# Measuring the Value of Resilience

*I don't measure a man's success by how high he climbs, but
how high he bounces when he hits bottom.*

—George S. Patton, Jr.

In 1999-2000, Xerox faced a weakening economy, a massive reorganization that didn't go very well, shrinking revenue, weak profits that cut shareholder stock value in half, and 19 billion dollars in debt. Customers were unhappy, employees defecting, and if that weren't enough, the company was under a worldwide SEC investigation for fraudulent financial practices.

According to Anne Mulcahy, former President and CEO, Xerox could have managed a few of these issues, but the cumulative impact was overwhelming. Was the company resilient enough to rebound? Did employees have what it would take to weather the storm? Would Mulcahy and her leadership team be able to maintain self-control, be proactive rather than reactive, and retain a calm focus? People were writing Xerox's obituary, but it made a remarkable comeback.

Communication and connection, while always important in an organization, become the number-one priority in times of crisis. Mulcahy's straightforward style and commitment to what she refers to as "the brutal truth"—her authenticity and willingness to be vulnerable—may have been one of the single most important factors in Xerox's recovery. At times like these, when leaders typically "go underground," and a veil of secrecy emerges around strategies and decisions, Xerox leaders were open and honest.

For most of her first year as President and CEO, Mulcahy traveled around the world, talking, and mostly listening, to employees and stakeholders. She invited employees to roll up their sleeves and be part of the recovery or leave. Her message, clear and simple: "Here's the problem. Here's the strategy. Here's how you can help." Mulcahy's humility and transparency trumped adversity, and loyal employees and customers worldwide united to rebuild Xerox's powerful presence.

To succeed, to excel, you need to build organizational resilience. That's the ability to quickly adapt to disruptions while maintaining continuous business operations and safeguarding people, assets, and overall brand equity.

We live in a time of relentless demand and extreme pressure. The pace of both work and life is faster than ever. We are bombarded by buzzing, pinging, ringing, tweeting, posting, Snapchatting, and Face-booking—a syndrome that fragments our attention while stealing our time and energy. Change is constant. Workplace stress and burnout are epidemic.

While we once were able to maintain a semblance of separation between work and home, nowadays there is an unavoidable bleeding of jobs into our personal lives. It has become normal to check email after dinner, before bed, and first thing upon waking. Whose idea was it to reach for the mobile phone at the sound of the alarm clock to check texts and emails before we greet the people we love? How did this become the new norm?

In his book, *The Turning Point: Creating Resilience in a Time of Extremes*, Gregg Braden, *New York Times* bestselling author and thought leader on bridging science, spirituality, and the real world, writes, "Our lives are changing with a speed that we've never seen, in ways that we're not prepared for, and faster than we've been taught to deal with. It's a new normal." Resilience, Braden claims, is critical to our ability to ride the winds of change and stand firm in the face of chaos and adversity. "We're living in a time of extremes ... resilience is our greatest ally ..." he says.

In this extreme world—where work and life seem to have merged, crisis is commonplace, change is constant, pressure is relentless, and stress is overwhelming—we must develop a new set of rules regarding the way we think about how we work.

## Resilient Individuals Make Resilient Organizations

When you are resilient, you are able to rebound, recover, and quickly bounce back from setbacks. You cope with disappointments and stress, overcome obstacles, and easily recover from or adjust to change or misfortune. You are proactive vs. reactive, controlling any egotistical expression and desire to be "right" and make others wrong.

Organizations are the same way, and that is no coincidence, considering that the lifeblood of any organization is its people.

For individuals and organizations alike, resilience is a mindset, skillset and toolset that provides a roadmap to maintain physical, emotional, mental, and relational health irrespective of the circumstances.

*"Since companies are made up of employees, for a company to be "fast, friendly, flexible, and focused," it obviously needs employees who possess these qualities. Workers who feel stressed out and overwhelmed don't. Resilient employees do."*

**– Rosabeth Moss Kanter, Professor of Business, Harvard Business School**

Like people, resilient organizations are able to quickly and effectively bounce back and recover from adversity. A resilient workforce is a productive workforce. A resilient workforce is healthy, energetic, durable, and enthusiastic. Employees remain engaged, focused, and productive. Truth telling, transparency, honesty, and vulnerability are valued. Trust remains intact because employees are informed about decisions and how they were reached. There is no secrecy about who is going, who is staying, and why.

In this environment, employees are "always apprised and never surprised" when a colleague is escorted out of the building. It's expected (but not celebrated) that companies engage in layoffs during times of turmoil or downturn. Courageous leaders avoid labor cuts at all costs, knowing that the backlash can be costly. In an environment of uncertainty and overload, the "survivors," i.e., employees who remain, tend to settle into a disgruntled malaise. Top talent may choose to go elsewhere while the remaining people hunker down and hope for the best, wondering who's next. It's no surprise that in these circumstances there is secrecy, resulting in apprehension and an erosion of trust. The outcome is the emergence of gossip and speculation.

While organizational leaders may expect remaining employees to be more productive to make up for the loss of their colleagues, that typically doesn't happen. Instead, added pressure leads to increased stress and burnout. It's the paradox of the weak organization—one that does not possess adequate resilience.

While the internal struggle and despair are evident to those inside the organization, external impact is often more significant. The brand equity of the organization is negatively impacted by gossip and storytelling, which creates a public perception that can take years and sizable resources to repair.

> *"When times are tough, employees at great workplaces show the resiliency to pull through. When times get better, those same employees are ready to lead the rally. It all adds up to cumulative success 2x better than the market average."*
>
> – **Great Place to Work Institute**

## Protecting Your Greatest Assets

It takes courage and commitment for an organization to place a priority on protecting its greatest assets—its people. The world-famous San Diego Zoo, operated by San Diego Zoo Global (SDZG), has done just that. It has created a world-class workforce through a sustained high-performance culture, organizational goals and drivers, a big-picture plan for the future, and numerous employee engagement programs. The result has been expanding global influence and success, anchored by a memorable experience for every guest. While it's not the perfect organization, it has been acclaimed for its forward-thinking philosophies and people-centric focus. SDZG was named the "Best Place to Work in San Diego," by the Society for Human Resource Management (SHRM), and many other organizations are turning to SDZG for help on various human resources best practices.

While "going for the roar" might be considered a playful take on animal behavior, at SDZG the concept of the "roar" is carefully woven through its strategic plan to create and sustain a workforce that is proud, committed, and fully engaged in its mission and vision.

When employees roar, you can see it in their eyes. You will observe it in their interactions with colleagues and guests. They are joyful, energized, polite, and helpful to colleagues and guests alike. With the roar comes the necessary creativity and energy to fulfill SDZG's vision to end extinction. The roar can build resilience in your organization as well.

### SDZG'S CORE VALUES: The ROAR

Make a difference for wildlife.
Share the wonder of nature.
Feel the passion for what we do.
Breed financial stability.
Succeed together.
Remember the roar...and pass it on.

Building resilience in an organization not only fosters a healthier, more productive workforce, but it also serves to build brand equity. SDZG is highly regarded in the international conservation community, recognized for its best practices in animal care and preservation. Its San Diego Zoo Global Academy is the recognized source for animal care education, as well as soft skill training and development. The SDZG Academy boasts over 125 member organizations, which equates to thousands of participants.

The Association of Zoos and Aquariums and the International Association for Amusement Parks and Attractions (IAAPA) have recognized SDZG as a leader in the attraction industry, and for its people practices. Tim and his team are asked to give presentations about SDZG's various HR programs and practices at various conferences around the country, including those for SHRM, IAAPA, WorldatWork, and many other organizations.

## Engaging Your Organization

How can you invoke a roar of passion, purpose, and commitment to fulfill your organization's vision and mission? You can do it by buying into a consciousness of caring, heart-based leadership—putting people first.

Building a resilient organization is not for the faint of heart. It requires courage, passion, and resolve, and you will need a clear roadmap to guide your systematic implementation of programs and resources. The goal is to integrate a mindset, toolset, and skillset that become woven into the DNA of the organization and stand the test of time.

The following chapters will provide you with tools, strategies, and practical ideas to help you build a resilience strategy that has a positive long-term impact on your business.

## Zoo Print for Success

❧ Examine your organization's level of resilience. Determine whether your employees are resilient enough to cope with the stresses, demands, and changes in your organization while remaining deeply engaged, highly productive, and wildly creative.

❧ Consider building a business case for implementing a resilience strategy. What will be the payoffs?

❧ Begin discussions about the importance of resilience and gain the support of key influencers.

## World-Famous Leadership Questions

❧ How resilient are you? Do you have the physical, emotional, and mental strength to bounce back from setbacks and remain calm in times of crisis?

❧ What kinds of behaviors do you demonstrate in difficult times?

❧ What is the potential cost or negative impact on your organization of failing to build adequate resilience?

## ROAR LOUDER

If you were to assume full responsibility, what action would you take to build a more resilient team or organization?

**CHAPTER**

# 2

# Building Resilience in Your Organization

*To win in the marketplace you must first win in the workplace.*

– Doug Conant, former CEO of Campbell Soup Co.

Building a resilient organization doesn't require heroic acts or elaborate initiatives that consume a great deal of resources. At San Diego Zoo Global, resilience begins with a commitment from senior leaders who articulate a compelling vision to honor and respect employees. Building on a strong "why," leaders establish a people-centric focus and implement a culture of resilience that becomes part of the organization's DNA. A well-designed strategy, combined with thoughtful programs, practical tools, and metrics to measure progress, transform how people behave, and recognize and reward resilient behaviors.

## The Resilience at Work™ Model

Many resilience models focus on stress management. While managing stress is indeed a critical factor, we believe that building resilience encompasses a broader spectrum of behaviors as reflected in the Resilience at Work™ model, (Figure 1.1). This model incorporates five competencies, referred to as the 5 Cs:

1. **Reclaiming Self-Control**

    *Your ability to self-regulate, self-manage, control your emotions, maintain clarity and focus, stay calm, be proactive vs. reactive, and be consistently optimistic and happy.*

    *Core behaviors:* Being self-aware; self-controlled; self-regulated;

empathetic; nonreactive; nonjudgmental; calm under stress or pressure; confident; certain; non-egotistical; optimistic.

2. **Realigning Conditions**

*Your ability to effectively integrate work and life, manage overall wellbeing and align external conditions to support effective use of time and energy.*

*Core behaviors:* Making healthy choices; managing overall wellbeing; coping well with stress; staying focused; managing time effectively; managing distractions adeptly.

3. **Reimagining Communications**

*Your competence and agreement with coworkers regarding truth-telling, honesty, commitment to transparency, acceptance of vulnerability, and focus on positivity.*

*Core behaviors:* Being positive; truthful; transparent; kind; authentic; willing to be vulnerable; solution-oriented.

4. **Renewing Connections**

*Your sense of purpose, connection, and coherence with personal and organizational values, feelings of belonging, trust, and support from your community.*

*Core behaviors:* Being aligned with corporate and personal values; connected with others; trusting; comfortable with conflict; a team player; vulnerable; supportive; collaborative.

5. **Rebalancing Commitments**

*Willingness to embrace change and commitment, adopt new habits, and implement new practices and rituals.*

*Core behaviors:* Embracing change; being comfortable with risk; being assertive; being persistent; being successful at adopting new habits; being courageous; and being a leader.

# Resilience at Work

A model for individuals and organizations to thrive in disruptive times.

Rebalance Commitments

Renew Connections

Reimagine Communications

Realign Conditions

Reclaim (Self) Control

*Figure 1.1. The Resilience at Work™ model incorporates five competencies.*

These 5 Cs are simple yet powerful. They are practical and universal. They apply to every person and organization, no matter the company size, industry, demographics, or culture. They are fundamental behaviors that serve everyone in creating more fulfillment and success at work and in life.

The Resilience at Work™ model seeks to combine tried and true concepts such as emotional intelligence, wellness, time management and good communication with a new perspective: mindfulness. Indeed, mindfulness is a tool to maintain relaxed, focused attention. Coupled with honest communication that promotes transparency and vulnerability; a sense of purpose, belonging, and connection; and the courage and conviction necessary to make resilience a priority; the model offers a road map to cultivate resilience in your organization.

The Resilience at Work™ model serves as a paradigm to reimagine the way we go about our jobs. It can help your organization meet its goals and objectives, and at the same time, safeguard your employees' quality of life. When each of these competencies is systematically integrated into the organization's culture, they foster a toolset that allows employees to thrive.

## Enhancing Financial Stability Boosts Resilience

The Dow Jones Sustainability Index defines corporate sustainability as "a business approach that creates long-term shareholder value by embracing opportunities and managing risks deriving from economic, environmental and social developments." One might argue that resilience provides an operational tool for recognizing, improving, and measuring corporate sustainability. While the Resilience at Work™ model focuses on human behaviors that constitute resilience, the corporation is responsible for ensuring financial resilience—the ability to embrace opportunities, manage risks, and thrive in disruptive times.

The zoo business is challenging, to say the least. At its core is an incredibly wide spectrum of animals who need individual care by experts. When it's too hot or too cold, the animals need special care and guests don't come. When times are tough, visitors are reluctant to pay for admission and donations often decrease. It's a labor- and capital-intensive operation. Zoo profits are typically invested directly back into upgraded facilities, better animal exhibits, and enhancing the guest experience.

In this kind of high-touch business, there are few opportunities to automate and save on costs. A small drop in attendance can have significant impact on the profit and loss statement. Therefore, long-term financial stability is key.

That is certainly the case at SDZG. As with all zoos, its leaders must be intently focused on how to survive and weather economic storms.

Revenue earned by SDZG from admissions and other operating sources is directed solely to keeping the facility going, including caring for the collection. All donations raised go to future exhibits and new experiences. For the past several years, SDZG's financial goal has been to be independent of donations. Its "one organization" mantra brings leaders from the Zoo, Safari Park, Institute for Conservation Research, Warehouse and Zoological Society of San Diego together to maintain and control expenses. Rather than competing with each other for resources, as has been the case in the past, now the leadership team collaborates to identify priorities, and all agree to "sink or swim" together.

"This perspective has served to break down historic silos, maneuvering and lobbying for resources," says David Page, director of finance and controller. "The shift in leadership from siloed to collaborative has created the context for leaders to focus on what will make the organization better as a whole."

## Producing Superior Financial Results

The shift to a more people-centric organization has had significant financial impact on SDZG. As employees have rallied behind the powerful mission, vision, and values, they have become more engaged, and as a result more creative and innovative, delivering an exceptional guest experience.

SDZG's CFO and leadership have developed a clear objective of ensuring long-term financial sustainability. Managers have been given tools and processes that allow for greater insight into financial drivers. With these tools, they have been able to make strategic decisions to keep the Zoo on the path to financial resilience.

Monthly executive updates include an in-depth review of the budget, income, and expenses, with an emphasis on teams working together for the greater good. The results have been dramatic. SDZG is posting record revenue and cash flow, which allows the organization to enhance its impact and invest heavily in capital maintenance.

At the same time, donations continue to rise, making it possible to invest more heavily in conservation, which is part of SDZG's vision to lead the fight against extinction, one species at a time. These support worldwide conservation efforts, including projects in nearly 80 different countries.

High focus on the guest experience keeps people coming in, and coming back. Through innovative pricing strategies, revenue per visitor has increased. Premium experiences such as the VIP Ultimate Safari, a one-day custom exploration including off-exhibit areas, animal interaction and a personal tour guide, enrich the visitor's experience while generating revenue beyond the average ticket price.

Animal care is obviously a priority at SDZG, with animal stewardship funds directed separately to the Zoo and Safari Park. Each fund receives $500,000 per year for projects that are devoted specifically for animal care. The result is a newfound respect between units that previously competed for resources. In the past, animal care groups and other operating units may have felt that funds devoted to the guest experience or operations resulted in a smaller piece of the pie for them—a zero-sum game. Now, all of SDZG's units work together with an understanding that a better overall guest experience results in additional funds.

## ZOOView

The Roar & Snore premium experiences offer sleepover adventures at the Safari Park, where guests relax in comfy tents surrounded by the sights and sounds of wildlife. Sleepovers include camp activities, an after-hours look at the "wild" life of the Park's animals, guided walks, a campfire program, dinner, an evening snack, and breakfast the following morning. Premium experiences like Roar & Snore have served to increase revenue while adding value to the guest experience.

## Knowing Your Cost of Low Resilience

This book will help you lead your organization to a high level of resilience. However, as with any journey, you can't get there without first knowing your starting point. In this case, you can determine where you are now by calculating your *Cost of Low Resilience (CLR)*.

Of course, everyone understands the financial concept of a bottom line, and you may remember your first day in accounting class when this formula was written across the board:

Revenue − Cost = Profit

Your professor may have exclaimed, "That's it! This is the basis to accounting." And, of course, he or she was right. In layman's terms, it means that a company's value is equal to its assets minus debts.

It is the same with resilience. Just as the Greeks invented double-entry accounting thousands of years ago with its system of debits and credits, we have standard inputs and measurements for an organization's resilience.

## The Resilience at Work™ Calculator

To calculate your organization's CLR, begin by determining your Resilience Score. To determine your resilience score, you will rate your organization on each of the five Resilience at Work™ competencies, then deduct costs, such as the cost of disengagement, turnover, and employee relations issues, as well as labor-related costs such as absenteeism, medical claims, workers comp expenses due to stress and ill health, the cost of customer dissatisfaction, and product and service quality.

**Step 1: RESILIENCE SCORECARD.** Enter a number from 1 to 5 that best reflects your organization's level of mastery in each of the five Resilience at Work™ competencies, where "1" represents incompetence; and "5" indicates a high level of competence. Your rating for each competency should reflect the behaviors demonstrated by the majority of employees on a consistent basis. High levels of mastery in each of these competencies add value to your organization. In order to gain more accurate ratings, you might consider administering the Resilience at Work™ assessment[1], or other similar assessments that measure resilience in the workplace.

| | |
|---|---|
| **1. Reclaim Self-Control** Employees' ability to self-regulate, control emotions, and remain calm under pressure. | |
| **2. Realign Conditions** Employees' ability to manage well-being, control distractions, and make wise use of time and energy. | |
| **3. Reimagine Communications** Employees' willingness to be honest, truthful, transparent, and vulnerable, particularly in times of stress. | |
| **4. Renew Connection** Employees' connection to the vision and values of the organization, sense of purpose, trust, partnership, and collaboration. | |
| **5. Rebalance Commitments** Employees' openness to change, willingness to adopt new habits, and perseverance. | |
| **6. Add lines 1-5** | |
| **7. Divide the number in line 6 above by 25** | |
| **This is your Resilience Score** | _____% |

[1] The Resilience at Work assessment can be found at www.Uexcel.com

A high score indicates your organization has the capacity to overcome challenges and thrive. It suggests you are able to remain agile and adaptable in the face of change, and effectively respond to demands and pressures to achieve goals while maintaining employee fulfillment. A low score suggests you haven't adequately developed the necessary mindset and behaviors in your organization to effectively deal with adversity, putting your company at risk.

**Step 2: COST OF LOW RESILIENCE.** Enter your organization's annual revenue, then calculate the Cost of Low Resilience based on the financial impacts identified below.

| 8. Your organization's annual revenue | $ |
|---|---|
| 9. Disengagement | $ |

Annual cost of loss of productivity due to disengagement.

Based on engagement research, the Human Capital Institute developed a model of what disengagement could be costing your organization. This model assumes that a person's salary is a reasonable measure of their value to the organization. Begin by using an engagement survey to identify the percentage of employees who are fully engaged, engaged, somewhat engaged, and disengaged. Next, work with your CFO to make some assumptions about the different returns on salary each level of engagement delivers. In these measures the return each level of engagement delivers relates to discretionary effort and therefore employee productivity. For example:

- Fully engaged employees return 120 percent of their salary in value

- Engaged employees return 100 percent of their salary in value

- Somewhat disengaged employees return 80 percent of their salary in value

- Disengaged employees return 60 percent of their salary in value

Use an average salary to calculate how much each employee at a given engagement level is returning to the organization. For example, if the average salary in your organization is $100K, you can calculate the value of a somewhat engaged employee as follows: $100K x 80 percent = $80K. The value returned by each employee is $80K – their salary ($100K) = –$20K, or a loss of $20K. Finally, to determine the cost of disengagement, multiply the value returned for each level of engagement by the number of employees who ranked at that level.

| **10. Employee turnover** Annual cost to recruit, interview, onboard, train and replace employees who were terminated or resigned. | $ |
|---|---|

Consider how many of your talented employees left in the last year. How much did you spend on training those employees? How much will you spend to train new employees? What does it cost you to attract, screen, interview and select new employees? What is the cost of lost productivity while new employees are getting up to speed?

| **11. Medical and health** Annual costs of health insurance, medical claims and worker's compensation for injury or illness, as well as cost of absenteeism. | $ |
|---|---|
| **12. Employee relations** Annual cost of labor and legal fees to resolve employee conflicts, complaints, and legal investigations. | $ |
| **13. Customer dissatisfaction** Annual cost incurred due to poor customer service resulting in loss of market share, loss of customers, and cost of customer acquisition. | $ |

| | |
|---|---|
| **14. Product or service quality** Annual cost of delays in production time, cost of repairs and warranty servicing, loss of sales. | $ |
| **15. Total Cost of Low Resilience** (CLR) Add lines 9 to 14 to calculate the total Cost of Low Resilience.<br><br>This represents the annual cost to your organization of chaos due to the lack of resilience. In other words, this is the amount of money being wasted by your organization. As you build resilience in your organization, this cost will decrease and you will increase margins. | $ |
| **16. Cost of Low Resilience Percentage** Total CLR as a percentage of annual revenue.<br>Divide the total in line 15 above by your organization's annual revenue in line 8. This represents the Cost of Low Resilience as a percentage of revenues. | % |
| **17. Optimal Resilience Score** A resilient organization has a Resilience Score of 90 percent or higher. | **90%** |
| **18. Resilience Deficit** The Resilience Deficit as shown in figure 2.1 represents the effort required to achieve optimal resilience. Subtract your current Resilience Score in line 7 from the Optimal Resilience Score of 90% in Line 17 to identify your Resilience Deficit. As you implement strategies to cultivate greater resilience in your organization, your Cost of Low Resilience will decrease, as will the Resilience Deficit. | % |

Here's an example of how to calculate your Resilience Deficit:

Your Resilience Score = 60%

The Optimal Resilience Score = 90%

Your Resilience Deficit = 90% - 60% = 30%

## The Resilience at Work Calculator

🐾 **Resilience Score:** Calculated using the Resilience Scorecard. *Sum of the 5C's (Resilience at Work competencies) divided by 25.*

🐾 **Cost of Low Resilience** (CLR): Financial impact of low resilience. Cost of disengagement; employee turnover; medical and health; employee relations; customer dissatisfaction; poor quality.

🐾 **CLR Percentage:** CLR as a percentage of an organization's annual revenues. *CLR divided by annual revenue.*

🐾 **Optimal Resilience Score:** A resilient organization has a Resilience Score of 90 percent or higher.

🐾 **Resilience Deficit:** The gap between the current level of resilience and the Optimal Resilience Score. *Optimal Resilience Score less Your Resilience Score divided by Current Resilience Score.*

## The Cost of Chaos

Chaos is the enemy of a great organization. Sadly, many organizations have become so accustomed to chaos that they don't even recognize it. At those places, chaos has become business as usual.

Chaos robs your organization of time, spirit, focus, and energy—your four most precious resources. It comes from a lack of resilience, unclear standards for behavior, and inability to effectively respond to disruption. Chaos sabotages your ability to fulfill your vision, mission and values, and provide a stable, productive work environment where employees thrive.

In her book, *The Outstanding Organization: Generate Business Results by Eliminating Chaos and Building the Foundation for Everyday Excellence,* Karen Martin says: "Left unchecked, chaos destroys everything that's good about an organization, its products, and the people who make them."[2]

## cha·os

**noun:** chaos; plural: chaoses
Complete disorder and confusion.

**synonyms:** disorder, disarray, disorganization, confusion, mayhem, bedlam, pandemonium, havoc, turmoil, tumult, commotion, disruption, upheaval, uproar, maelstrom, muddle, mess, shambles, free-for-all, anarchy, lawlessness, entropy

**informal:** hullabaloo, hoopla, train wreck, all hell broken loose

One unfortunate business phenomenon is that successful companies can fail when they encounter disruption. When faced with threat of a competitor's new product or technology, a downturn in the economy or an internal crisis, revenue declines, top talent leaves and stock values tumble. Some companies recover after costly restructuring and painful downsizing, but many don't.

The root of the problem often isn't an inability to take action, but a lack of resilience—the absence of the necessary mindset, skillset and toolset to ride the winds of change and avoid chaos. An organization that is able to maintain calm, focus on the positive, and be honest and transparent, while harnessing the creativity of its human resources, is much more likely to survive and thrive under pressure.

"Leading companies can become stuck in the modes of thinking and working that brought them their initial success," explains MIT Sloan School of Management lecturer, Donald Sull. "When busi-

---

[2] Martin, Karen, *The Outstanding Organization: Generate Business Results by Eliminating Chaos and Building the Foundation for Everyday Excellence*, McGraw-Hill, 2012

ness conditions change, their once-winning formulas instead bring failure."[3]

Most companies know what to do to overcome the challenges they face. They have the necessary knowledge, expertise, and resources to win. So why do they fail when faced with change? Look what happened when oil prices hit an all-time low of $40 per barrel in 2014-2015. Some oil and gas companies initiated widespread layoffs and intensive cost-cutting measures to protect shareholder interests.

The plummeting price of oil ripped into the U.S. energy industry so dramatically that the oil sector laid off 87,000 people in 2015. Chevron announced that it would lose between 6,000 and 7,000 jobs—the second four-figure round of dismissals at the company since July 2015, according to *The Guardian*.

As with the oil crisis in the 1980s, fear and uncertainty caused panicked decisions and reactive responses that provided short-term benefit and long-term consequence. Most importantly, the fabric of trust in these organizations was damaged. In the 1980s, when oil companies engaged in widespread layoffs, it dissuaded college students from pursuing careers in petroleum engineering, resulting in a shortage of skilled workers. While the financial benefits of working in the oil and gas industry are attractive, instability and lack of loyalty may steer engineers into alternate areas of specialty, leaving the industry scrambling for qualified talent when oil and gas prices recover.

At a time when communication is needed more than ever, the opposite seems to happen during disruptive times. Secrecy prevails, transparency disappears, and tight-lipped, behind-closed-door conversations become the norm. Gossip spreads as employees speculate, trying to anticipate decisions. Old patterns and processes—"the

---

[3] Donald Sull and Kathleen M. Eisenhardt, *Simple Rules: How to Thrive in a Complex World,* Houghton Mifflin Harcourt, 2015

way things have always been done"—blind leaders from creating new pathways. Ego takes control, causing people to posture, manipulate, and lobby in order to protect their positions. The easy "wrong" takes precedence over the hard "right." Employees are left feeling disoriented and disenfranchised as they begin covert job searches.

The spirit of creativity and innovation that is critical for the organization to pull through is compromised. When a culture of resilience exists, organizations are better equipped to weather the storms of change and emerge triumphant.

## Zoo Print for Success

- ❧ Calculate your organization's resilience score and the impact on profits. Identify opportunities for improvement.

- ❧ Analyze the behavioral patterns in your organization that might have contributed to an inability to effectively handle change, crisis, or adversity in the past.

- ❧ Develop guidelines for behavior when disruption strikes.

## World-Famous Leadership Questions

- ❧ Is your organization financially resilient? If not, what needs to be done to build financial resilience?

- ❧ What patterns of behavior in your organization will protect you from failure?

- ❧ What patterns of behavior will put you at risk for failure or collapse?

## ROAR LOUDER

If you had the opportunity to redesign the way in which your organization responded to change in the past, what would you do differently?

## CHAPTER
# 3

# Implementing Resilience the World-Famous San Diego Zoo Way

*Human resources isn't a thing we do. It's the thing that runs our business.*

— Steve Wynn, Wynn Las Vegas

The human resources and talent management programs developed by San Diego Zoo Global have revolutionized its worldwide influence and success by mapping closely to the principles of organizational resilience, providing a successful model that any organization can follow. However, ideas alone won't get the job done. They require leadership and follow-through to achieve their full potential.

In 2004, SDZG had an opening for a chief human resources officer. Through a series of referrals, and coincidences, the nationwide search for this key position led to someone in their own backyard. That person is the co-author of this book, Tim Mulligan. Back then, Tim happened to live a few blocks from the San Diego Zoo. He had been working as a human resources leader for Starwood Hotels & Resorts for the previous eight years—four years in San Diego, and before that, had stints in San Francisco and Seattle.

While working for Starwood, Tim became known as a go-to guy for the implementation of new and exciting programs throughout the organization. These included college relations, customer service training, and union negotiations, as well as various benefit, performance management, and recruiting programs. This was what the Zoo seemed to be looking for—someone who could shepherd in a new era of people practices; someone who could bring new ideas to the table, and usher this 88-year-old nonprofit organization of several thousand employees into the modern world.

Immediately upon taking this new position, Tim observed that the general employee population of SDZG was, on average, very long-tenured. Many employees had worked there for years, mainly because they loved the mission of the organization and were very passionate about the natural world. However, the organization was never really regarded as an employer of choice, and was sorely lacking in some basic infrastructure that would support fully engaged employment. People did not stay because of the people programs—they stayed because of the animals.

Fortunately, Tim started his new position just as SDZG was rolling out a very strong strategic plan—"The Lynx." This embodied a new vision for the organization: to become a world leader at connecting people to conservation. To achieve this vision, SDZG realized that it had to become a leader in world-class employee relations programs and talent management.

## Seeking to Become World-Class

At the time Tim came on board at SDZG, the organization lacked the basic elements of talent management. It had no performance management program, a lack of formal employee training and development programs, a lack of reward and incentive programs, and inconsistency in management policy application. There was no formal compensation program to speak of. The human resources team, which had remained very resilient over the years despite limited budgets, had not made the optimal organizational connections and partnerships needed to succeed with best-in-class employee programs.

Amidst all of this, there seemed to be a real desire for change. When Tim first polled the management team on wish lists for training topics, he was overwhelmed with the responses. When he and other senior executives scheduled meetings to discuss the way forward, the rooms were filled to capacity; employees and managers were hungry to learn and change. The executive team did not need much arm-twisting to buy into new concepts—all seemed to agree that change needed to occur for SDZG to be known as a world leader.

## Enter The Lynx: A Resilient Approach

SDZG's new strategic plan, dubbed The Lynx, was heavily weighted to core infrastructure programs—accountability, basic foundations, and bringing employees to the forefront. It ushered in a new vision of becoming a world leader in connecting people to wildlife and conversation. Developed by over 170 employees, The Lynx focused on creating a new infrastructure at SDZG, and repositioning the organization as a global conservation leader. The original Lynx had four main components focusing on facilities, interpretation, conservation, and supporting processes—with the latter being the playing ground where Tim and the HR team had to start over in all areas of human resources. It was a challenge that Tim was very excited to lead.

Instead of just jumping in and making sweeping changes ad hoc, the HR team did things the right way. They worked within The Lynx to prioritize the needs of the organization. A few very big ideas needed attention right away—namely, performance management, employee engagement and satisfaction, and training. Others on the list were "shelved" for future years—including recognition, incentive, and wellness programs, as well as college relations and other recruiting efforts.

## Performance Management

Prior to 2005, SDZG had a robust budgeting program, with inherent goals in basic metrics such as attendance, fundraising amounts, revenue, and profit. But these goals were never transparent—they never were communicated to the larger population of employees.

There were no goals set for the management team or hourly employees that were linked to the annual goals of the organization. There was no formal compensation program to govern annual raises and bonuses. New hires were brought in as low in the pay scales as possible, and whenever annual increases were given, there was no correlation whatsoever to pay or goals. No incentive plans existed.

In 2005, as part of the Lynx Strategic Plan, SDZG established a special team charged with finding the right partner to help develop a cutting-edge online performance management program. While this search was taking place, the management team of SDZG was polled on leadership competencies in order to create a common language and set of expectations for anyone who managed at least one employee. Whether you were a food service supervisor of hundreds, a marketing manager, an animal care manager, or even the CEO, you would be held accountable to a common set of competencies.

Ultimately, the team selected an up-and-coming Canadian vendor named Halogen Software. SDZG and Halogen began working together on a strategic performance management project that would encompass these principles. Halogen led a team of SDZG managers in creating the program, which included the creation of the SDZG Leadership Competencies (Leadership, SDZG Mission and Customer Focus, Professionalism, Teamwork: Interpersonal Relations, and Communication), as well as a merit-based compensation program—a first for SDZG.

## Z-Max Transforms Organizational Culture

The fall of 2005 saw several turning points in SDZG's transformation to the next level of strength and organizational resilience. First, the executive leadership team created a set of nine goals for 2006, including those for groups not previously measured, such as animal welfare, conservation, employee relations, and training.

SDZG then launched the new project developed by Halogen Software, the first of many to be "branded" by the SDZG human resources team with its own catchy name and logo: "Z-Max." An overarching theme of the original Lynx strategic plan was on leadership accountability, for which Z-Max would play a major role. Managers were trained on the basics of writing "SMART" goals—those that were Specific, Measurable, Attainable, Realistic, and Time-bound. They then conducted reviews based on those attributes, and annual increases were finally tied to individual performance.

Finally, the management team was speaking the same language, and all eyes were on the same prize. Employees were able to see their role in the success of the organization, whether working in janitorial, retail, or any department and position.

Z-Max was the first of many programs to come that ushered in modern technology to the organization, driving managers away from old school paper-based programs, and toward online paperless technology.

Now, 10 years later, Z-Max has truly transformed the culture of SDZG. There is a sense of accountability, a better understanding of goals, and stronger motivation for employees to become productive and engaged. What started out with 225 participants now has grown to 850. Currently, all non-union employees are given annual goals and held to a set of competencies. They have individual development plans and "360 reviews" by peers, managers and their own direct reports, and are rewarded accordingly. In 2015, the first group of union employees was added to the system as well, with more to come in the future.

Though there were costs for creating this program, SDZG leaders made a strong business case on the importance and relevance to the Lynx; future returns in terms of productivity and accountability; higher engagement; and the risks involved in not proceeding. The funds were approved. This initiative boosted the productivity, and yes, the resiliency of the organization, which more than justified the financial investment.

## Living and Working by the Rules of Engagement

An effective brand is embodied in products, services, people, and guest experiences. SDZG's positioning as "World Famous" places it uniquely in the market, communicates the organization's values, and is a measure of its success. Ideally, each member of the management team becomes an accountable leadership brand ambassador. This includes incorporating SDZG's code of conduct for all employees: the "Rules of Engagement," a set of simple yet powerful standards for behavior based on the premises of Sandy's previous book, Excellence at Work: The Six Keys to Inspire Passion in the Workplace.

As shown in Figure 3.1, the Rules of Engagement are:

**1. Use your word wisely.**

 🐾 We think and speak about what we want to have happen.

 🐾 We communicate clearly and often.

 🐾 We avoid the "downward spiral" and 3 "C's"—criticizing, condemning, and complaining.

**2. Be accountable.**

 🐾 We take full ownership and responsibility.

 🐾 We look for what WE can do to improve situations.

### 3. Focus.
❧ We focus on what's important and use our time and energy wisely to achieve our goals.

❧ We stay 100 percent engaged at work.

### 4. Mine the gold.
❧ We bring out the best in ourselves and others.

### 5. Strive for balance.
❧ We are healthy, energized, and vital.

❧ We take time for recovery and renewal.

❧ We sharpen our "saws" —stay engaged and at the top of our game!

### 6. Lighten up.
❧ We remember not to take ourselves so seriously!

❧ We bring laughter, joy, and fun to our workday.

❧ We are constantly making other people's day.

### 7. Go for the Roar.
❧ We delight every customer, always wear a smile, and give GRRREAT customer service!

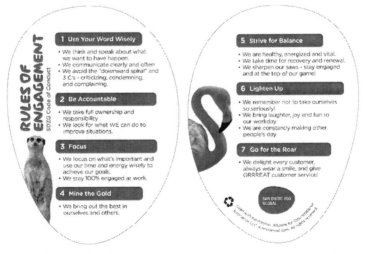

*Figure 3.1. SDZG's Rules of Engagement are a set of simple yet powerful standards for employee behavior.*

Z-Max programs also incorporate SDZG Leadership Competencies, SDZG Success Competencies (for all employees), as well as mentoring, collaboration, and advocacy. These modules have been designed to provide pertinent information specifically branded to the SDZG leadership team, and to teach skills that will have an immediate, lasting impact.

## Zoo U Spurs Professional Development

 Before the introduction of The Lynx strategic plan, SDZG had relied on the creativity of its departmental managers to handle training. There were no organizationally sponsored programs for onboarding, internal management training, succession planning, or customer service training. Nor was there any form of leadership development program for its management team. That all changed in late 2004 with the advent of Zoo U. Now, 10 years later, Zoo U has become an industry-recognized platform for training on all levels, with at least 20 core programs that have been developed in-house, including:

- **Roar Louder Series:** In late 2004, when Tim polled the SDZG leadership team on desired training topics, he was overwhelmed with the multitude of suggestions. These ranged from management basics (i.e., basic supervisory skills, time management, and conflict resolution) to industry-specific (i.e., conservation projects, animal welfare, and nonprofit governance) to more advanced topics (including legal training, budgeting, and coaching). These ideas spurred the monthly Roar Louder program.

- **Roar Stronger Series:** This spinoff of the successful Roar Louder Series is composed of four quarterly programs geared to SDZG non-management employees. Employees are incentivized to attend at least two of the four programs, and hundreds choose to go to all four. Geared toward creating stronger and more engaged employees, sessions focus on financial or health wellness, introducing new organizational programs, or providing timely information on a range of other topics of professional interest.

❧ **Extraordinary Leadership Training Program:** When Zoo U was created, Tim promised to SDZG management team members that they each can expect to go through a leadership development program at least every four years. The operational concept is that strong leadership at all levels is the key to business success, and the best leaders are lifelong learners.

❧ **Executive Leadership Development Program:** This year-long program prepares SDZG's current and future executives to translate leadership excellence into winning business results.

❧ **Exceptional Leaders Program:** This is a series of cutting-edge online leadership courses, coupled with three in-person meetings for reflecting upon what was learned and sharing best practices.

❧ **GRRREAT! Customer Service Training:** Being one of the top tourist destinations globally, it is obvious that customer service needs to be at the forefront for SDZG. Tim recognized this need, and put a team together to create this mandatory training program for all current employees, as well as all new hires.

Chapter 17, "Raising Leaders," provides details on Zoo U's programs and their impact on SDZG's resiliency.

## Rewards and Recognition

This is where things really got fun for the organization. One major initiative in The Lynx strategic plan was to create a well-rounded rewards and recognition program, with an expected rollout of one new program component per year over five years. This became the SDZG Roaring Rewards program. Created by a team of representatives from a range of departments, Roaring Rewards now has set a new bar for other organizations, and in fact has won several awards itself. The five award programs include:

- 🐾 **Zooper Market:** To innovatively and creatively address the issue of rewards and recognition on a tight budget, the human resources team created this internal performance incentive and appreciation program. SDZG managers have money allotted to their departments, go online to the "Zooper Market" for a menu of choices, and do some online shopping for their employees. The HR department fulfills the orders.

- 🐾 **Zooper Stars:** This program recognizes employees, nominated by their managers, who embody the organization's core values.

- 🐾 **Zooper Heroes:** These supervisors and managers, voted upon by their peers, embody the organization's core values.

- 🐾 **Zooper Troopers:** These are the SDZG years of service awards.

- 🐾 **GRRREAT! Work:** This is SDZG's peer-to-peer recognition program, whereby employees can recognize each other for great work and exhibiting extraordinary customer service, via a ticket system, which yields cash rewards.

❖ **Zooper Bowl:** All of these awards are celebrated at the quarterly Zooper Bowl, attended by the SDZG senior management team.

## The Roar Back! Employee Satisfaction Survey

Tim feels very strongly that regular surveying and reactions to surveys are key to measuring employee engagement and satisfaction. When he began at SDZG, he learned that employee satisfaction had not been measured in nearly two decades, making it very difficult to "get a pulse" on what the employees were really thinking about as they dedicated their talents to SDZG. So, SDZG created a team to fix this. With such a specific and unique culture and essentially no budget, an off-the-shelf program definitely wasn't the way to go. Instead, the team created its own custom solution. One group worked on the technology, drawing on the expertise of the marketing department, and in particular, the organization's web team. Another group worked on the content of the survey. As a result, the Roar Back! Employee Satisfaction Survey was born.

The survey covers 12 competencies:

1. Feedback
2. Teamwork
3. Quality and Customer Focus
4. Mission and Purpose
5. Compensation
6. Workplace and Resources
7. Opportunities for Growth
8. Work-Life Balance

9. Fairness

10. Respect for Management

11. Respect for Employees

12. Communication.

The Roar Back! Survey is administered online once a year, during Employee Appreciation Month in October. The results are quickly communicated to managers, who then are required to submit a Roar Back Action Plan for the 12 months leading up to the next survey, based on the results. Managers are held accountable for their departmental scores through Z-Max.

With each survey report there are separate scores for satisfaction and engagement, with training dedicated to help everyone properly distinguish between the two characteristics. Roar Back Action Plans now address each department's areas of improvement.

The Roar Back scores are at an all-time high. Much emphasis has been placed on this process, and the employees now trust the program, and see it as an important change vehicle. It is another best practice that has not only helped sculpt SDZG's culture, but has enabled ongoing positive changes based on each year's results.

## Building Resilience

These are just a few of the core programs that have been put in place to improve the overall employee experience, and make SDZG a true employer of choice. As each new program is implemented, Tim has his team ask the ever-important question/mantra: "ITWF, which stands for "Is This World Famous?" If the answer is no, then it's back to the drawing board. In addition, with each new program, Tim makes sure that not just the CEO, but the entire executive team is on board with the new initiative, supports it publicly, and rallies around the rollout.

## Zoo Print for Success

❧ How effectively do your HR practices help to build organizational resilience?

❧ Where do your HR processes fall short?

❧ What are your organization's rules of engagement?

## World-Famous Leadership Questions

❧ How satisfied are you with your employee satisfaction and engagement scores?

❧ To what degree does your rewards and recognition program provide meaning and value?

❧ How effectively does your training program develop the necessary skills to build resilience?

## ROAR LOUDER

If you were to consider your HR practices to be the trim tab that helps stabilize your organization and build resilience to run at an optimum level, what would you do differently?

## PART TWO:

# Reclaiming Self-Control

The foundation of resilience is self-control—the ability to self-regulate, self-manage, control your emotions, maintain clarity and focus, be proactive vs. reactive, and be consistently optimistic and happy.

The first of the 5Cs, self-control, enables you to more effectively respond to stress and demand, make better decisions and minimize the negative effects of egotistical behavior. When you have a high level of self-control, your behavior is more consistent. You are less likely to be triggered by fear of loss of control, false pride, or a need to be right. That helps you cultivate trust and loyalty.

Using functional magnetic resonance imaging (fMRI), scientists studying self-control have found that the prefrontal cortex—the part of the brain that controls executive function, such as planning and making choices—is more active in people with greater self-control. Self-control enables you to filter out distractions so that you can plan, focus attention, remember instructions, and juggle multiple tasks successfully. It enhances clear, rational thinking, and the ability to see yourself and your changing circumstances objectively. It helps you to make decisions that serve you well in the long term.

Organizations that exhibit a high level of self-control are better equipped to weather change, and respond thoughtfully to adversity. They are less encumbered by worn-out processes and fixed ways of doing things, and therefore less likely to react inappropriately. They demonstrate an increased ability to maintain a calm focus on what is most important, foster good relationships internally and externally, and remain optimistic.

CHAPTER

**4**

# Looking Inside Yourself

*Everyone thinks of changing the world,*
*but no one thinks of changing himself.*

— Leo Tolstoy

Look into the fifth-grade classroom at Glendale Elementary School after recess, and you will find kids seated in a circle practicing mindfulness. In collaboration with the Center for Investigating Healthy Minds at the University of Wisconsin-Madison, teachers incorporate a 10-minute mindfulness practice after lunch—a time of day when kids are typically rowdy and distracted. After meditating, teachers find that students are calmer, more focused, and better able to learn. The hip-hop song, "Don't Flip Yo' Lid" by JusTme, has made meditation cool for these fifth graders, who chant the mantra, "Deep breath so you don't make a mistake," as a reminder to control their emotions and treat classmates with kindness and respect.

Our lives are filled with distractions. The demands and pressures to do more, faster, better have left us feeling overwhelmed. Our minds are agitated, our attention is fragmented, and our ability to be present in the moment is compromised.

A mind that is calm and relaxed is better able to solve problems, make decisions, and respond thoughtfully. As a society, we have recognized the importance of physical exercise to manage stress. Now it's time for us to train our minds, to be able to calm down at will.

More people are recognizing this imperative, which is why mindfulness is slowly becoming more mainstream. Increasingly, corporations are embracing mindfulness training or meditation practice, providing courses, spaces, and opportunities for employees to center themselves, find clarity and become more compassionate. For example, Google and many other progressive organizations offer their employees free meditation classes, along with health club memberships and other perks.

Business schools, like Claremont Graduate University and Harvard Business School, are also teaching students about mindfulness, the *Wall Street Journal* reported. The *Journal* explains the case for mindfulness training like this: "While the idea of mindfulness originates in the serious practice of meditation, B-school faculty say it has many applications for executives who aren't looking for a spiritual fix, but simply want to clear their heads and become aware of reflexive, emotional reactions that can lead to bad decisions."[1] The deeper your meditation experience, the more likely you are to exhibit higher emotional intelligence and lower perception of stress.

## ROARING IDEAS

Led by Chade-Meng Tan (job title: Jolly Good Fellow), Google introduced a scientifically backed program to increase emotional intelligence using mindfulness. It's called "Search Inside Yourself" and is now offered to organizations outside the Googleplex.

## Developing Self-Control

How well do you self-regulate, manage your response, and react to stressors? Do you take the time to think through things and empa-

---

[1] Business Skills and Buddhist Mindfulness: Some Executive-Education Professors Teach Ways Students Can Calm Their Minds, Increase Focus, *Wall Street Journal*, April 2012

thize with other people before jumping to conclusions? Are you able to distance yourself in the heat of the moment and pause before reacting? *Response flexibility* is the name for the ability to pause before you act when you experience a strong stimulus instead of reacting habitually. You are able to pause for a split second, which gives you choice in how you react to the situation.

*"Between stimulus and response, there is a space. In that space lies our freedom and our power to choose our response. In our response lies our growth and freedom."* – Viktor Frankl[2]

Self-control is the ability to calm your mind, train your attention, and maintain peace and tranquility, particularly in difficult times. Success at this depends on your level of emotional intelligence, or EQ, and the degree to which you are able to break free of your ego, "... the endless craving for respect, vanity, praise, and flattery, and the ceaseless indulgence of selfish desires."[3]

To reclaim control of your true self requires a wholehearted commitment to serve others, to share and make the greater good a priority. "This shift is the transformation from 'I' to 'we,' the most important process leaders go through in becoming authentic," says Bill George, Harvard Professor, former CEO of Medtronic, and best-selling author. "How else can [leaders] unleash the power of the organizations unless they motivate people to reach their full potential? If our supporters are merely following our lead, then their efforts are limited to our vision and our directions. Only when the leaders stop focusing on their personal ego needs are they able to develop other leaders."[4]

---

[2] Frankl, Viktor E., *Man's Search for Meaning*, Beacon Press, 2006 (not first edition)

[3] Berg, Michael, *Becoming Like God, Kabbalah and our Ultimate Destiny*, Kabbalah Publishing, 2004

[4] George, Bill, *True North: Discover Your Authentic Leadership* (Hoboken, NJ: Jossey-Bass, 2007).

## Leading Without Ego

Leadership without ego is a rare commodity. When leaders get caught up in false pride or self-doubt, it erodes their effectiveness. That's because ego gives people a distorted image of their own importance. When you lead with ego, you put your own agenda, safety, status, and gratification ahead of you. "World-famous" leadership—the kind of leadership people long for—requires humility, the desire to bring out the best in others. Jim Collins talks about this in his classic book, *Good to Great*. Collins suggests there are two characteristics that describe great leaders: *will* and *humility*. Will is the determination to follow through on an organizational vision, mission, or goal that is bigger than you are. Humility is the capacity to recognize that leadership is about serving others instead of being served.

When self-serving leaders are experiencing success, they look in the mirror, beat their chests, and tell themselves how good they are. When things don't go well, they look outward and blame everyone else. On the other hand, when things go well for "world-famous" leaders, they look out the window and give everyone else the credit. When things go wrong, "world-famous" leaders look in the mirror and ask themselves, "What could I have done differently?" That requires real humility.

"I don't have to be the smartest person in the room just because of my job title," says Dwight Scott, director of the San Diego Zoo. "I do have to bring out the best ideas from each person on any given project. And that's really what's important for the organization. It's not about me. It's about our work. I've learned I'm not usually the smartest person in the room. We all have our own style and strengths. I just bring out the best in everyone else. It's back to 'Mine the Gold' in the Rules of Engagement."

Scott can be regularly seen walking the Zoo with a warm smile, greeting employees, asking them what they're working on, engaging them in dialogue about their accomplishments. For Dwight, and other leaders at SDZG, their priority is recognizing others' successes and progress toward ending extinction, rather than self-aggrandizement.

Benjamin Zander, conductor of the Boston Philharmonic Orchestra and international speaker, has a unique practice to bring out the best in his orchestras. When Zander notices musicians are disengaged, he asks himself, "Who am I being that the eyes of my orchestra players aren't lit up?" Zander has a practice of placing a blank sheet of white paper on the music stand of every musician he conducts. With the blank sheet comes the invitation for orchestra players to make requests, offer feedback, and provide Zander with insight that will make him a better conductor.

If you were to place a blank piece of paper on each of your employees' desks with a request for feedback on how you could be more effective, what would they say? Do you have the courage and humility to take their feedback to heart, to look inside yourself and make the necessary adjustments to relinquish egotistical behavior and serve the greater good of your organization?

## ROARING IDEAS

In every building on the General Mills campus outside Minneapolis, MN, there is a meditation room, equipped with a few Zafus—cushions for sitting practice—and yoga mats where employees can grab a few minutes of equanimity in between meetings.[5]

---

[5] Gelles, David, The Mind Business, *FT Magazine*, August 24, 2012

## Nurturing Strong, Stable Attention

Strong, stable attention leads to calm and clarity. The way to train your attention is through the practice known as mindfulness meditation. According to Jon Kabat-Zinn, Professor of Medicine Emeritus and creator of the Stress Reduction Clinic and the Center for Mindfulness in Medicine, Healthcare, and Society at the University of Massachusetts Medical School, mindfulness is "paying attention in a particular way on purpose, in the present moment, and nonjudgmentally."[6]

Research suggests that by meditating regularly, the brain is reoriented from a stressful fight-or-flight mode to one of acceptance, a shift that increases contentment.[7] Research from Carnegie Mellon University has become the first body of work to demonstrate that even brief mindfulness meditation practice—just 25 minutes a day for three consecutive days—can mitigate psychological stressors.[8]

Published in the journal *Psychoneuroendocrinology*, the study investigates how mindfulness meditation affects people's ability to be resilient under stress. It can be challenging to sustain mindfulness in times of stress or trauma, but when you do, you are able to stay calm and consistently infused with tranquility and serenity. This leads to greater optimism and happiness, which builds resilience.

Just as you are training your body to become stronger and more flexible when you go to the gym, meditation training enables your mind to gain greater flexibility and strength. The more you prac-

---

[6] Kabat-Zinn, Jon, *Wherever You Go, There You Are: Mindfulness Meditation In Everyday Life*, Hachette Books, New York, 2005

[7] Lutz, A., Greischar, L., Rawlings, N.B., Ricard, M., Davidson, R.J. Long-Term Meditators Self-Induce High-Amplitude Synchrony During Mental Practice. *Proceedings of the National Academy of Sciences* (2004), 101, 16369-16373.

[8] Creswell, J. David, Pacilio, Laura E., Lindsay, Emily K., Brown, Kirk Warren, Brief Mindfulness Meditation Training Alters Psychological And Neuroendocrine Responses To Social Evaluative Stress, *Psychoneuroendocrinology*. June 2014, Vol. 44, pp. 1-12.

tice, the stronger the mind becomes. When you bring mindfulness and attention to your work you are more present and focused with people. You listen more attentively without your mind wandering and settling into judgment. Mindful listening is a very powerful way to build trust and create connectedness.

*The most precious gift we can give others is our presence. When mindfulness embraces those we love, they will bloom like flowers.*

— Thich Nhat Hanh

## Mindfulness: A Core Competency

Whether or not you face danger in your work, your ability to remain calm and focused in any circumstances builds resilience. SDZG animal keepers bring a high degree of mindfulness to their work in order to minimize risk when feeding animals, cleaning their enclosures, or simply tending to their needs. Even animals that seem cuddly can use their teeth, so keepers must always stay alert. A lesser cat, such as a serval or caracal, is only two or three times the weight of a large domestic cat. Their instincts and background, however, make them aggressive enough to kill a small antelope or flamingo. A high level of alertness and concentration, combined with relaxed, calm focus, helps keepers be aware of unusual animal behavior or impending danger.

The giant panda seems like a very innocuous animal when observed in the Zoo, yet anyone who encroaches on its territory will find it more than willing to defend itself, and a human can be seriously injured. Gao Gao, SDZG's 24-year-old male giant panda, is no exception. During breeding season, keepers and veterinary staff track his blood pressure with great care and competency. Equipped with apples cut into bite-sized pieces, a bucket of biscuit balls, bamboo bread, and a blood-pressure monitor attached to an extension cord, panda keepers and veterinary technicians get into position. As Gao Gao heads into the squeeze cage, an area used to administer medications to some animals, he plunges his arm into a secured steel sleeve. "We use this sleeve to collect blood samples," explains Brian, a registered veterinary technician at the Zoo. "He knows to hold onto the bar inside the sleeve. To get his blood pressure, we just wait a few minutes for him to let go of the bar and let us place the cuff around his forearm." All the while, Gao Gao is being hand-fed his favorite snacks.

As the bottom of the treat bucket becomes visible and his blood pressure readings have been duly noted, a keeper puts a few drops of rubbing alcohol on the floor and the bear happily rolls around on it. "Usually animals balk at the scent of rubbing alcohol, but Gao Gao loves it—it's like catnip to him," explains Brian. "It's the ultimate treat!" With the procedure completed, Gao Gao is free to mosey back out on exhibit.

"We are fortunate to have such highly trained keepers who understand how to handle these animals safely," says Liz, the panda keeper. "They always remain alert and mindful at work in order to provide the best care possible."

## Interpersonal Mindfulness

The practice of being mindful and attentive with animals extends to interpersonal relationships at SDZG. President and CEO Doug Myers takes time with employee representatives from each department on a quarterly basis to listen to concerns, questions, and ideas. Myers is known to be an attentive listener, welcoming of feedback to inform his communication strategy. No topic is off limits. His ego-less leadership style creates an openness and trust that serves the greater good. "Doug isn't consumed with personal gratification or reputation," says Dwight Scott, Zoo director. "His priority is how we can provide the best possible guest experience while fulfilling our vision. As leaders, we understand that in order to accomplish this, we must be open-minded and humble."

## Building Emotional Intelligence

Emotional intelligence (EQ) is one of the best predictors of success at work, and for fulfillment in life. It's a key component of resilience. Peter Salovey and John D. Mayer, the researchers who developed the model of EQ, define it as "… the ability to monitor one's own and others' feelings and emotions, to discriminate among them, and to use this information to guide one's thinking and actions."[9] These skills aren't necessarily innate. Anyone can become more emotionally intelligent.

Daniel Goleman, a thought leader in the study of EQ, reported an analysis that shows emotional competencies comprise 80 percent to 100 percent of the distinguishing competencies of outstanding leaders.[10] No one can control all feelings perfectly, but we all need some emotional control. When people are frequently overwhelmed by emotion, it affects their judgment and ability to make decisions. They also find it more difficult to get along with others and recover when they are upset.

In his books, *Emotional Intelligence: Why It Can Matter More than IQ* and *Working with Emotional Intelligence*, Daniel Goleman presents five categories of EQ:

1. **Self-awareness:** People who are emotionally intelligent have a healthy sense of self-awareness, understand their own strengths and weaknesses, and how their actions affect others.

2. **Self-regulation:** Those who have high emotional intelligence are better equipped to manage their emotions and exercise restraint when needed.

[9] Salovey, Peter and Mayer, John D., Brackett, Marc A, *Emotional Intelligence: Key Readings on the Mayer and Salovey Model*, National Professional Resources, Inc. / Dude Publishing, 2004
[10] Goleman, Daniel, *Working with Emotional Intelligence*, Bantam, 2000

3. **Motivation:** Emotionally intelligent people are self-motivated. They are usually resilient and optimistic when they encounter disappointment and are driven by an inner ambition.

4. **Empathy:** A person who has empathy has compassion and an understanding of human nature that allows him to connect with other people on an emotional level. The ability to empathize allows a person to respond genuinely to others' concerns.

5. **People skills:** People who are emotionally intelligent are able to build rapport and trust quickly with others on their teams. They typically win the respect of coworkers.

How much of an impact does emotional intelligence have on your success as a leader? A lot! TalentSmart®, the world's premier provider of EQ education, tested EQ alongside 33 other important workplace skills, and found that it is the strongest predictor of performance, explaining a full 58 percent of success in all types of jobs.

## Zoo Print for Success

- Assess your team's ability to demonstrate self-control. How developed is their self-awareness? What is their level of emotional intelligence?

- Identify how well your employees manage themselves in disruptive times.

- Develop a plan to infuse your organization with greater calm, tranquility, and relaxed focus to build resilience.

## World-Famous Leadership Questions

- How well do you self-regulate, manage your responses, and react to stressors, thereby cultivating greater resilience?

- Do you take the time to think through things and empathize with other people before jumping to conclusions?

❧ Are you able to distance yourself in the heat of the moment and pause before reacting?

## ROAR LOUDER

Consider inviting your team to offer anonymous thoughts, ideas, and feedback on how you can be more mindful, attentive, and consistent in your behavior.

CHAPTER
**5**

# Leading in a Way that Will Be Followed

*Make your ego porous. Will is of little importance, complaining is nothing, fame is nothing. Openness, patience, receptivity, solitude is everything.*

– Rainer Maria Rilke

How you lead is how you'll be followed. At San Diego Zoo Global, leaders are known for their integrity, kindness, and respect. This is how they attract employees and supporters for their cause. It's also how they bring humility and civility to everything they do. The assumptions employees make about what is acceptable or not comes from observing your leadership behaviors. In fact, as a leader you are scrutinized all of the time, especially when you think others are not looking.

Leading by example sounds easy, but few leaders are consistent in this regard. Every action, each conversation, is sending a signal to every person involved in your organization about the Rules of Engagement. Consequently, successful leaders practice what they preach. They know that everyone is watching their every move, and they assume full responsibility for their actions.

The SDZG Roar Back! employee satisfaction and engagement survey contains several statements focused on this subject. Regarding respect for employees and managers alike, employees are polled annually on the following statements:

❖ The management staff within my department treats me with respect.

❖ SDZG respects its employees.

❀ The management staff within my department values my talents and the contributions I make.

❀ I respect the management staff within my department as competent professionals.

❀ Our executive team members demonstrate strong leadership skills.

On the most recent 2015 Roar Back! survey, all of these questions polled at all-time highs. When the first Roar Back! survey was conducted in 2005, the statement on respecting the management team scored a dismal 50 out of 100. Since that was the first employee survey that had been conducted in 17 years, the executive team was stunned and disappointed. In response, SDZG put in place a plan to raise the executive team's visibility, and hopefully turn around the lack of respect and trust the survey had uncovered. This included, but was not limited to:

❀ executive teams being scheduled to visit departments they had not interacted with in the past

❀ executive team members spending full days in different departments, working alongside the employees

❀ pictures, names, and backgrounds of all executive team members put on posters that are hung on all communication bulletin boards around the facilities

❀ roundtable employee meetings facilitated by various executive team members

❀ a push to improve and increase the amount of transparent communication coming from the executive team.

The results have been resoundingly successful. Since 2005, positive responses to statements indicating mutual respect between executive teams and employees have jumped by 50 percent.

## A Commitment to Excellence

"I'm usually the guy in meetings reminding everybody about the Rules of Engagement," says Zoo director Dwight Scott. "The others go along with it, but they think I'm giving them a hard time. They are probably right." Scott is passionate about great leadership. He expects his team to lead by example, to set the tone for the rest of the organization, and to abide by simple standards that ensure everyone is treated with kindness and respect.

"The Rules of Engagement provide a framework—a structure of sorts—a playbook to steer and guide us. They hold us to the highest standard of conduct." Scott says. "After all, we are ending extinction. To do that, we have to manage ourselves in every moment. We've got to stay focused on our mission. Everything else is just a distraction."

"Leadership has always been of great interest to me," says Scott. "When I accepted the role of Zoo director, I was thrilled to find out we had the Rules of Engagement." According to Scott, the Rules of Engagement establish the tone for a positive working environment, and set the direction for leaders at all levels.

When asked what his leadership philosophy is, Scott replies by saying, "I try to keep things simple. I don't have any secrets. I smile at people. I acknowledge them. I thank them for what they do. I listen to them. I treat them well. I'm genuinely concerned about how they're doing. I recognize the role they have in making our organization work. I think these types of behaviors engender trust and respect. I always tell my leadership team to be the type of manager they've always wanted to work for."

A commitment to excellence requires courage and discipline. As the adage goes, excellence is a decision you make once, and a choice you make a thousand times. You may make the decision to lead by example, to excel, and yet every day your decision will be challenged by unconscious patterns, stressful circumstances, or difficult people. You must consciously choose excellence in every moment. When you are committed to excellence, you kick complacency, rebel against resignation and cynicism, and constantly challenge the status quo.

"Every zoo has lions, tigers, and bears," says Doug Myers, SDZG president and CEO. "What makes us really special are the people we have. It's the commitment to excellence at every level of the organization." At every level and in every department of the organization, what stands out is the way employees maintain the animal collection. "We have a strong commitment to animal care and welfare. In order to be global leaders in animal care, we must have a commitment to excellence in the way we lead our people too."

Committing to excellence calls for self-reflection—an unyielding candor with yourself. You are relentlessly disciplined in consciously choosing behaviors that engender respect and build credibility. In the face of stress, demand, pressure, or conflict, the choice to succumb to poor behavior becomes intolerable. When you relapse into less than admirable patterns, you are quick to admit your weakness and authentically ask for forgiveness. You don't permit yourself to sink into smugness based on past success. You have an unwavering drive to keep evolving.

Members of the SDZG managerial team (more than 300 and growing) are all trained on the Rules of Engagement, and how they can impact the culture using this code of conduct, as well as seeing that they are followed in all respective departments. Within the Z-Max talent management program, each manager is now reviewed annually on the SDZG Leadership Competencies, which contain elements of the Rules of Engagement. In addition, each manager is reviewed mid-year on the progress of his or her annual goal completion. All managers have a goal that is tied to talent management—either raising engagement and satisfaction scores, focusing on training and employee development, or success planning/career management.

"Some of SDZG's leaders are world-renowned. They are known for their integrity and leadership skills," says Beth Branning, corporate director of vision, innovation, and strategy. Bob Wiese, Ph.D., and chief life sciences officer, is known in the zoological world for his knowledge of animal care and conservation, coupled with business expertise. He leads global efforts to regulate animal breeding agreements globally, and chairs the Conservation Breeding Specialist Group that oversees management of animal programs.

"Wiese is an example of a leader who has a worldwide reputation in our business," Branning explains.

## Respect Benefits Everyone

Demonstrating respect doesn't just benefit you, it benefits everyone around you. No leadership behavior has a more significant impact on employee commitment and engagement.

A study of nearly 20,000 employees around the world, conducted by *Harvard Business Review* in conjunction with Tony Schwartz, confirmed that respect had the most significant effect on employees—even more important than recognition, appreciation, communicating the vision, and providing feedback. Respect rated even higher than opportunities for learning growth and development.

Employees who feel respected are 55 percent more engaged. They also report 56 percent better health and wellbeing. Eighty-nine percent report greater enjoyment and satisfaction with their jobs, and 92 percent report increased focus and prioritization. Those who feel respected by their leaders were also more likely to stay with the organization than those who believe respect was lacking.

## Roaring Ideas

A SHRM study found 72 percent of workers rank "respectful treatment of all employees at all levels" to be the most important factor in job satisfaction.

Showing employees respect can transform company culture and turn a business around. Doug Conant, former CEO of Campbell's Soup, is a great example. When Conant took over the leadership role in 2001, sales were in decline and the company had lost half its market value. Some commented that the level of engagement at Campbell's Soup was the worst seen among the *Fortune 500* companies. Conant transformed the culture in large part by showing employees respect. During his tenure as CEO, he wrote more than 30,000 personal notes of thanks to his 20,000 employees. He sought every opportunity to connect with people and express his appreciation for them. The results confirmed the impact of his leadership approach. By 2010, employees were setting all-time performance records, including outpacing the S&P five-fold.[1]

The key to mastering respect begins with increased self-awareness. There is never an excuse for being disrespectful. The more aware you are, the more you're able to adjust your behaviors. Small acts of kindness and respect can have big payoffs. They trickle down into your organization, and benefit everyone involved. "Respect has been deeply ingrained in the SDZG culture," explains Myers. "We never forget where we came from—we respect our past, and we take full responsibility for our future."

[1] Conant, Douglas, and Norgaard, Mette, *TouchPoints: Creating Powerful Leadership Connections in the Smallest of Moments*, Jossey Bass, 2011

"When Doug Myers says something, it's meaningful to the people. They very much respect what he has to say," says Ted Molter, chief marketing officer. Myers has a reputation for fairness and ethical behavior. He is willing to make hard choices that reinforce his commitment to SDZG's cause. "Myers is well respected by the Association of Zoos and Aquariums leaders, SDZG trustees, volunteers, and employees alike," Molter continues.

Leaders like Myers, Wiese, and Scott have high morals and display utmost integrity. The result: they are respected in the broader community where they take on important roles in charting the future of zoos, aquariums, theme parks, and even museums.

"Having served on committees and boards for several industry associations, I have realized that San Diego Zoo Global is always invited to be at the leadership table, primarily because we are respected and recognized for our conscious leadership," says Molter.

## Integrity Is Evergreen

Success will come and go but integrity is evergreen. Integrity means doing the right thing in every moment, even when nobody's watching. Doing the right thing requires courage and discipline, and appreciating that doing the right thing may have consequences. Building respect and integrity can take years, but it only takes one word, one action, to lose it.

It's easy to justify the means with the end. We live in a world where it has become acceptable to over-promise and under-deliver, to exaggerate and to overstate. Covering up mistakes has become commonplace. In each case these behaviors seem to have perfectly valid reasons why the result justifies the lack of integrity. Compromised integrity can cause chaos. It feeds distrust and indifference. It weakens the fabric of an organization.

Integrity is a core competency of a resilient organization. Without it, your organization is compromised at its foundation. As Warren Buffett, Chairman and CEO of Berkshire Hathaway says, "When hiring people, look for three qualities: integrity, intelligence, and energy. And if they don't have the first one, the other two will kill you." Tolerating lack of integrity in any form communicates an acceptance of it. That's why every violation of integrity must be addressed. You are known by the company you keep. Therefore, surrounding yourself with people of integrity, and rooting out those who lack it, is key to your success. President Dwight D. Eisenhower said, "The supreme quality for leadership is unquestionably integrity. Without it no real success is possible, no matter whether it is on a section gang, a football field, in the army, or in an office."

## Roaring Ideas

Dr. Fred Kiel[2] collected data on the integrity of 84 CEOs over a seven-year period, comparing employee ratings of CEO behavior to company performance. Kiel found that high-integrity CEOs had a multi-year return of 9.4 percent, while low-integrity CEOs had a yield of just 1.9 percent. What's more, employee engagement was 26 percent higher in organizations led by high-integrity CEOs.

Integrity is holding oneself to a high standard because it is the right thing to do. Leaders with integrity don't brush things off. They have a relentless sense of self-imposed responsibility to uphold the highest standards. "Myers and his team are known for their adherence to moral and ethical principles," says Branning. "Internal and external stakeholders know they can count on them to consistently conduct themselves with high ethical standards, honesty, and moral character."

---

[2] Kiel, Fred, *Return on Character: The Real Reason Leaders and Their Companies Win*, Harvard Business Review Press, 2015

## Stay Humble

One of the hardest things for leaders to do is to stay grounded in the face of a success. When people look up to you, defer to you, and associate the success of your organization with your decisions, it is tempting to believe that you have all of the answers. Ego is a trap. You can easily be blinded by the grandeur of past accolades, and in so doing fail to realize the importance of continual drive to earn your success. Once you concern yourself more with the joy and success of others—with the accomplishment of a cause that extends beyond you—you break free of your ego.

Being known as "world famous" has become a moderate point of pride and brand attribute for those who work at SDZG, but its leaders are conscientious about not allowing that tag to foster arrogance or breed ego. "When someone refers to us as 'world famous', I say thank you, it's nice to hear that," says Molter, "but we don't spend marketing dollars to tell people that." Rather, he believes that SDZG must work to earn that reputation every day.

"It's important we never take our brand for granted," Molter says. He even acknowledges that having a recognizable brand can sometimes be a detriment. "We have to stop once in a while and recognize what we've done, remind ourselves of the accomplishment, but we go about it with humility," he explains. "We want to do good. We want to make good choices because it's the right thing to do."

Reinforcing the brand reputation is accomplished subtly. "We focus on who we are, what we do, and our mission," Molter explains. "Sometimes we may use the tagline 'no wonder we're world famous', as an understated reinforcement."

## Zoo Print for Success

❧ Assess the assumptions employees make about what is acceptable and not acceptable from observing leadership behaviors in your organization.

❧ Identify any negative impact unacceptable behavior has on your organization's ability to succeed.

❧ Develop a strategy to elevate leadership behavior by establishing clear standards and expectations.

## World-Famous Leadership Questions

❧ How do you demonstrate respect for people in your organization?

❧ In what ways are you respected?

❧ How have past successes blinded you?

## ROAR LOUDER

Where have you demonstrated lack of integrity? What are you willing to do to restore lost trust?

CHAPTER
**6**

# Leading from the Heart

*People do not care how much you know until they know how much you care.*

– John C. Maxwell

In our corporate culture and society in general, the metaphor of the heart is often associated with weakness, giving in, or conceding power. Yet, in ancient times it was believed that the heart served as the core of human passions. Considered the universal center of emotions, it has always been seen as the most vital part of a person, the place where the depth and authenticity of an individual's feelings and words are born. The symbol of the heart alludes to a person's deepest essence, their most vulnerable point, the origin of his or her enthusiasm.

A heart-centered approach to leadership allows you to reflect before reacting. When you lead with the heart, not just your head, you are able to empathize with others, and respond to their needs to be valued and respected. "By acknowledging and honoring the human element, heart-centered leaders possess the wisdom and capacity to positively transform any organization and run extremely successful and profitable businesses," says Susan Steinbrecher, author of *Heart-Centered Leadership: Lead Well, Live Well.*[1] According to Steinbrecher, research confirms that companies led by heart-centered leaders have demonstrated unequivocal financial success. Qualities such as kindness, humility, and compassion lead to self-aware, conscious leaders—those who create a positive work environment and contribute to the bottom line.

---

[1] Steinbrecher, Susan and Bennett, Joel, *Heart Centered Leadership: Lead Well, Live Well*, Sustainable Path Publishing, Second Edition (January 28, 2014)

## Caring and Compassion

Creating a compassionate, caring organization begins with hiring the right people—those who are inherently kind and compassionate. Those who choose to work for San Diego Zoo Global do so because its mission and vision are aligned with their personal values, and because they are committed to making a difference in the world of conservation. Rather than outsource retail, food, and transportation services, as other organizations often do, the Zoo chooses to hire its own staff to perform these tasks. With every job performed by an internally selected team member, SDZG continues to build a family-like atmosphere. Employees, in turn, extend this caring and compassion to guests.

"Caring and compassion for animals and plants is non-negotiable," says Bob Wiese, the Zoo's chief life sciences officer. "We only hire people who love animals and nature. We do this to ensure we create a caring and nurturing environment for all species."

One reflection of compassion at SDZG is its renowned commitment to animal welfare. SDZG employees are encouraged to report any animal welfare concerns to a supervisor or the animal care management team by submitting a report to a seven-member Animal Welfare Panel (AWP), which is charged with collecting and analyzing data to ensure each animal thrives and has the best life possible. The panel provides evidence-based metrics leading to best practices, and responds to issues and concerns. Its guiding principle is providing animals "opportunities to thrive."

Cynthia, a Zoo employee, recounts her recent visit to the Harter Veterinary Hospital at the Safari Park as a part of the Visit-A-Job program. "I chose the hospital to learn more about the work our staff does with wild animals at the Park," she says. "I feel really proud to be part of the San Diego Zoo Global team. Our vets, techs and keepers really take good care of our animals. Animal welfare is clearly a passion and priority for all of them."

## ZOOView

The Visit-A-Job program is an internal initiative to promote professional growth, foster collaboration, and develop big-picture thinking. It encourages SDZG employees to visit other departments and work alongside coworkers to learn new skills.

Just as the welfare of animals and plants is a priority for SDZG, so, too, is the welfare of its workers. SDZG's Roar Safer program includes safety incentives, injury case management, preventative maintenance, training, and safety representatives for different departments. The Safety Committee is made up of supervisory representatives from each department who meet quarterly. Committee members receive training and tools, including the San Diego Zoo Global Academy's broad catalog of online safety classes, as well as a DIY course tool that allows them to create best-practice training for their specific departmental needs. One manager in each department is deemed a Safety Representative, with accountability goals for keeping the theme of safety alive within their work group all year long. Quarterly parties are awarded to departments exhibiting safe practices. And, at the end of the year, SDZG gives away a Smart Car to a winning participant in the Roar Safer program.

The commitment to caring and compassion for animals transfers to the people side of the business. Gather in a room with SDZG leaders, and you notice they are down to earth, unpretentious, and genuinely caring. War-like metaphors such as "crushing the competition" or "being bigger and better" are replaced with "do the right thing for the right reasons," "be generous with others," and "because it fulfills our purpose."

When asked, "Why do you like working for SDZG?", new hires, tenured employees, and those who have departed from the Zoo say things such as, "My friends and family are happy that I am part of an organization like this," or "What is there not to like? It's a pleasure to work for a world-class organization that is constantly on the cutting edge in all aspects of its operation."

## ZOOView

The 2014 Roar Safer goal was to incur fewer than 40 injuries that resulted in lost time. Thirty-nine injuries were reported. Employees in departments that met quarterly safety commitments were entered into a raffle for a Roaring Rewards party and two lucky safety leaders won Vespa scooters.

Paige, an entomologist, shares this story of how Zoo employees lead with their heart.

"A while back, I received a frantic email from a colleague: her eight-year-old nephew had been grappling with aggressive brain cancer, and she was planning a Make-a-Wish visit to the Zoo. She reached out to me hoping that we could help arrange a last minute behind-the-scenes tour. Every single coworker that I called on replied to this last-minute request with an 'Absolutely!' or 'What time works best for you?' We zipped from area to area over the entire day and the little guy had the experience of a lifetime! The staff in the Children's Zoo, Insect House, polar bears, giraffes, camels, education, elephants, and pandas made Will's day very special. Sadly, a few months later, he lost his battle with cancer. Upon my return from an overseas trip recently, a package filled with some very special thank yous awaited me. Inside was a poster depicting many of the special moments that Will experienced with our staff, and a note of gratitude; one for each area that we visited. It was a beautiful reminder of the incredible potential we have to touch people's lives, and how willingly we give our time to those in need. My most sincere thanks go out to the entire team of people who came together to make it happen—I am very proud to work alongside you."

## A Different Kind of Leadership

Caring and compassion go beyond day-to-day interpersonal exchanges to sometimes tough decisions that impact the bottom line. During the 2008-2009 recession, SDZG president and CEO Doug Myers and his leadership team decided there would be no layoffs. While attendance and revenue were down, SDZG stood firm in its decision to protect jobs. At the first-of-its-kind all-hands meeting, Myers announced that rumors about pending layoffs were false. To a resounding roar of applause, he promised a full house of employees that if everyone worked together to contain expenses and cut back wherever possible, they would get through it together.

"This was one of the boldest decisions our management team made," says Myers. "The payoff was significant. By extending compassion and respect to our employees, we have been repaid tenfold with increased trust and loyalty. This is a true family."

An open mind and heart fosters a conscious organization. This requires a different kind of leadership than is typical in corporations, one that is more servant-based, a leadership that is committed to serving the greater good and creating value for all stakeholders. "That person will need to have a higher level of emotional intelligence than we have traditionally found in business leadership," says John Mackey, CEO of Whole Foods. Mackey and his team have created a Conscious Leadership Academy, where leaders build emotional and spiritual intelligence. It prepares leaders to lead from a place of service by engaging them in experiences that help them to identify their higher purpose and create meaning in the workplace.

Higher purpose and meaning, while inherent in SDZG's mission and vision, are never taken for granted. SDZG's values and core tenets are reinforced at every meeting and in every publication. "Remember the ROAR and pass it on" is declared daily, with pride and respect for the legacy that Dr. Harry began in the early 1900s. It has become deeply ingrained in the culture, and serves as a reminder to all staff why they come to work every day—to continue the legacy.

## Roaring Ideas

Whole Foods' Whole Planet Foundation demonstrates caring and compassion. It provides affordable small loans to over 800,000 women in poverty across 61 countries, enabling them to start their own businesses. The money comes from customer donations and Whole Food suppliers.

## Fear: The Enemy of Accountability

Some organizations motivate through fear and control, manipulating employees to do things to avoid negative consequences. When people are frightened, uncertain, or feel insecure, their creativity is stifled, and their desire to add value beyond the basic requirements of their job is suppressed. In a fear-based work environment, employees often duck their heads, attempt to go unnoticed, and play it safe. Punishment precludes employees from stepping up, speaking out, or trying something new. On the other hand, when fear is removed, people are more willing to take risk, tell the truth and go the extra mile.

## GRRREAT News

Compliments and comments from guests and coworkers about employees who go the extra mile are highlighted in SDZG's publication, *GRRREAT News*. There is only one rule for *GRRREAT News*—that it's all good news.

"The *GRRREAT News* publication keeps us upbeat and aware of our accomplishments, while recognizing and rewarding Rule of Engagement number two: 'Be Accountable'," says Becky Lynn, SDZG director of employee communications. "It's my favorite communication piece. It has helped develop a culture of positivity by constantly reminding us that despite the challenges, we have many things to celebrate."

SDZG employees are willing to go beyond job expectations and take ownership, even when it's not their responsibility.

*"I want to make sure Justin, zoo buildings and grounds attendant, knows how much I appreciate his assistance in giving the Kopje exhibit a much-needed facelift. I was just looking to borrow his vehicle to tow the power washer over to the enclosure. Well, Justin went many steps above and beyond! He picked up the power washer with me, helped me set it up in the enclosure, asked the crew to power wash the rockwork surrounding the Kopje exhibit, not just one morning, but two! His willingness to help at the drop of a hat was an unexpected surprise that really contributed to the improvements made to the area."*

– Lisa, **Animal Care Manager**

## Courage and Accountability

In CBS's *60 Minutes* report, "Alone On the Wall," free solo rock climber Alex Honnold scaled Half Dome, a granite mountain face, rising nearly 5,000 feet above the valley floor in Yosemite National Park, California. Honnold made the steep ascent, pausing occasionally to wipe the sweat from his brow and dip his damp hands in a bag of chalk strapped to his waist. With no rope, regular climbing shoes, and no room for error, he scaled a 2,000-foot vertical face with relaxed focus and total control.

Honnold's renown transcends the climbing realm. He is one of the most famous adventurers in the world. His accomplishments have much to teach us about risk, reward, and the ability to maintain focus even in the face of extreme danger. Above all, he offers a framework for accountability.

When you're alone in a challenging situation, as Honnold is while following his passion, there is no one to blame, and nobody is going to come along and bail you out. It's all up to you.

How do you create a similar mindset in your organization? How do you instill full responsibility and full accountability for every action and outcome? How do you inspire creativity, risk-taking, and innovation that elicit satisfaction? How do you engage employees in going beyond the call of duty, not because they were forced to, but because they chose to?

If you want the people in your organization to overcome the natural tendencies to make excuses and dodge accountability, you must establish trust, eliminate fear, and reward risk and failure.

## Roaring Ideas

*"A thin line separates success from failure, the great companies from the ordinary ones. "Below The Line" lies excuse making, blaming others, confusion, and an attitude of helplessness while "Above The Line" we will find a sense of reality, ownership, commitment, solutions to problems, and determined action."*

**– Roger Connors, CEO, and New York Times bestselling author of *The Oz Principle***

## Establishing Clear Ground Rules

When individuals, teams, or organizations deny responsibility, blame others for the way things are, or throw their hands up in helplessness and hopelessness, there is a price to be paid. According to Roger Connors, CEO and *New York Times* bestselling author of *The Oz Principle*,[2] this price often includes poor results, failed initiatives, missed targets, and poor morale. On the other hand, when the work environment is designed for accountability, it will flourish.

Accountability ground rules are a framework you can use to address this in your organization. (See Figure 6.1.) These are a clearly defined and well-articulated set of principles that govern how people respond to tough situations. In Figure 6.1 you will find ideas you can build on to design meaningful ground rules for your team. By engaging your employees in this process and inviting them to devise the rules, compliance will likely be greater, and peer accountability will create a self-policing process.

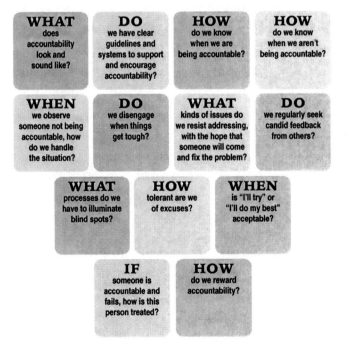

*Figure 6.1. Accountability ground rules can inspire creativity, risk-taking, innovation, and productivity.*

[2] Connors, Roger, Smith, Tom, and Hickman, Craig, *The Oz Principle: Getting Results Through Individual and Organizational Accountability*, Portfolio; Revised Edition, 2004

## Authenticity Breeds Trust and Loyalty

"Authenticity" is the new buzzword in the business world. Leaders are taught to be open, honest, and to share personal stories to gain trust and build loyalty. Authenticity begins with self-awareness: knowing who you are—your values, emotions, and competencies— and how you're perceived by others.[3] To be authentic is to be genuine. True authenticity doesn't require you to tell others who you are and what you value, because they are able to see what you value from the way you lead, the way you treat others.

It requires courage to be authentic, to be open and connected, to invite questions, concerns, and criticism—and to respond to these genuinely and honestly. "SDZG's Communications Action Group, which includes representatives from every area of the organization, meets with CEO Doug Myers, Tim Mulligan, and me prior to each quarterly Open Forum to talk about concerns or suggestions they hear in their day-to-day activities," explains Becky Lynn, director of employee communications. Open Forums are held at all five locations, including ICR, the off-site retail warehouse, and administrative offices, so that all employees have an opportunity to hear updates on important conservation projects, operational issues, and other important news. "Nothing is off limits," Lynn says. "Myers and other leaders take questions and suggestions on any topic, which are then published in the employee newsletter."

With authenticity comes freedom and acceptance of vulnerability. "In our culture we associate vulnerability with emotions we want to avoid such as fear, shame, and uncertainty," notes scholar, author, and public speaker Dr. Brené Brown. "Yet we too often lose sight of the fact that vulnerability is also the birthplace of joy, belonging,

---

[3] Rosh, Lisa, and Offerman, Lynn, Be Yourself, But Carefully, *Harvard Business Review*, October 2013

creativity, authenticity, and love." In her TED talk on The Power of Vulnerability, Dr. Brown dispels the cultural myth that vulnerability is weakness, and reveals that it is, in truth, our most accurate measure of courage.

Steve Jobs, Warren Buffet, Eleanor Roosevelt, and Oprah Winfrey are examples of leaders who exemplify authenticity by speaking openly, and sometimes disclosing personal frustrations, fears, and failures. At his commencement address at Stanford University in 2005, Jobs stated, "Truth be told, this is the closest I've ever gotten to a college graduation." He went on to explain why he dropped out of college, describing a series of failures on his journey to the success of Apple Inc.

Warren Buffet admits that his $200 million purchase of Berkshire Hathaway was his biggest mistake. Eleanor Roosevelt displayed candor in her autobiography revealing shortcomings. One of her famous quotes is, "People grow through experience if they meet life honestly and courageously. This is how character is built."

Oprah Winfrey, too, has been open about the trauma she faced as a child. As Brené Brown puts it: "Authenticity is a collection of choices that we have to make every day. It's about the choice to show up and be real. The choice to be honest. The choice to let our true selves be seen."[4]

According to the Conference Board of Canada, authentic leadership helps build resilience in organizations during times of uncertainty. "Authenticity contributes to the level of trust and confidence people have in their leaders and to employee engagement, performance, and productivity," says Maureen Brown, senior facilitator at The Niagara Institute.

---

[4] Brown, Brené, *The Gifts of Imperfection: Let Go of Who You Think You're Supposed to Be and Embrace Who You Are*, Hazelden, 2010

## Zoo Print for Success

❧ Engage in a discussion with leaders in your organization about how to create an environment where people feel safe and secure, an environment where people feel cared for and respected.

❧ Identify ways in which leaders can demonstrate more caring and respect for employees.

❧ Examine your team's accountability "ground rules." Where are there opportunities to clarify and articulate clear standards and expectations for accountability?

## World-Famous Leadership Questions

❧ Do you lead from love or fear?

❧ Do people who work with and for you really know you? How authentic are you?

❧ How is fear manifesting in your organization?

## ROAR LOUDER

How can you remove fear from your organization and create a more caring, compassionate workplace where people feel fully valued and respected?

## PART THREE:

# Realigning Conditions

Realigning conditions builds on the foundation of self-control to increase your ability to effectively integrate work and life, and manage overall wellbeing and external conditions to support effective use of time and energy.

At the 2014 World Economic Forum, wellbeing became a macro issue, put on the agenda for large multinational CEOs and governments worldwide. The new imperative is for companies to move from a mindset of managing risk related to health, to one where health and wellbeing enable business. Wellbeing is a catalyst that companies need to build resilience. It cultivates engaged employees who perform at their best every day.

Gallup's research reveals that when companies add a wellbeing component to their engagement initiative, it has an accelerating effect. According to Gallup, "in a company that supports employees' wellbeing and engagement, workers are more likely to be thriving overall, which helps boost their individual, team, and organizational performance."

---

[1] Heifetz, Justin and Wood, Jade, "Memo to Executives: Wellbeing Boosts Employee Engagement," Gallup Research, December 2014

Disruption takes a toll on individuals and organizations. In order to maintain wellbeing, it's necessary to perpetually adjust and realign both inner and outer conditions. Inner conditions relate to physical, intellectual, emotional, and spiritual health—those conditions over which you have control. Outer conditions, which will be addressed more in depth in Chapter 9, include external circumstances or the work environment—the culture, processes, and structures that either respect and support resilience or detract from and diminish your team's capacity to remain focused and accomplish their most important goals.

CHAPTER
# 7

# Making Wellbeing a Priority

*People who are mentally, physically, and emotionally hardy are better able to grow from the harsh tests of life. Such individuals seldom feel victimized by circumstances and tend to learn more from challenges and stay healthier along the way.*

– Robert K. Cooper, *The Other 90%*

Greatist's 44 Healthiest Companies to Work For in America identifies organizations that are "redefining office culture and proving that working hard and finding balance aren't mutually exclusive." An online community that is devoted to promoting healthy choices, Greatist highlights workplaces that go beyond the token bowl of mushy apples in the meeting room to strategic wellbeing initiatives that promote overall health. Today's savvy workers place a priority on these types of organizations. In response, forward-thinking companies are bolstering their employee value proposition by offering robust programs that include not only healthy food options and fitness programs, but also premium services such as medical care, massage, laundry, car wash, bike repair, haircuts, and dry cleaning, to name a few.

## Employee Health: The Roar Longer Wellness Program

Once you build a resilient workforce, you need to maintain it. Recognized as one of the Healthiest Companies in 2014 by the *San Diego Business Journal*, San Diego Zoo Global has found a way to ensure that employees remain engaged in their own wellbeing, which, in turn,

makes for a healthier staff and subsequently a more resilient organization. This holistic approach is encompassed in SDZG's Roar Longer
wellness program, which supports Rule of Engagement #5: Strive for
Balance.[1] It consists of nine facets encompassing many tools that can
be used by employees to track and improve their health. These tools are
mainly technological while the programs are hands-on, both taking
the program above and beyond the standard wellness program.

SDZG provides employees with an online portal through which
they can keep track of their individual (and confidential) health scores.
These scores are acquired through various point-based activities,
including two that, if eligible participants take part, will also offer
a discount on their health insurance. This additional incentive motivated 85 percent of eligible employees to participate by answering
a health risk assessment questionnaire and taking a biometric
screening test. The results are only shared with the employee, but the
true outcome is a knowledgeable staff member who may otherwise
not have gotten this annual check-up.

Further opportunities for points come in the form of fitness
contests such as walking and healthy eating—all self-reported, as
well as discounted "boot camp" classes to improve healthy habits,
eye and dental exams, book clubs, meetings with a certified financial planner (paid for by the company) to improve financial health,
and sharing health recipes on the web portal. The points gained
qualify employees for quarterly and annual prizes including elec-
tronic pedometers and  spa trips.

In addition to tracking wellbeing and promoting healthy living,
Roar Longer provides much-needed assistance when an employee's
health is compromised due to an injury or illness, utilizing a workers'
compensation program, Zero Time Loss, and various medical leave

---

[1] SDZG's Rules of Engagement are based on the Six Keys to Excellence, and are used with permission of Alliance for Organizational Excellence LLC

programs. Each of these rich benefits comprises not only state and federal mandates, but also offers additional advantages to each eligible employee. These include supplemental pay when someone is out of work on a medical leave, or temporary, productive job tasks that a worker can perform outside of his or her regular job when an injury or illness limits them. This obviously relieves employee stress brought on by fear of job-loss or the inability to contribute.

The final segment of the Roar Longer wellness program, the education component, covers all other portions simultaneously. SDZG human resources consistently arranges educational opportunities for all staff members. Through classes in the Wellness Portal or My Academy, along with Roar Louder supervisory training, Roar Stronger staff training, and health and retirement fairs, education is at the forefront of this successful program, empowering employees to take charge of their own health.

## ZOOView

SDZG employees who earn points for participating in the annual biometric screening event, Health Risk Assessment, and other wellness activities are entered into quarterly raffles for healthy lunches, mountain bikes, Whole Foods gift cards, and a stay at Rancho La Puerta, a world-class fitness and spa retreat.

## Wellbeing: More than Counting Steps

When thinking about wellbeing, too many companies focus primarily on physical health and neglect to address the whole person, which is why so many wellness programs fail. To have a positive impact on employees' wellbeing, you must move beyond simply counting steps with an app or tallying pounds lost in a weight-loss challenge, to embrace all the components that contribute to an employee who thrives. This means putting wellbeing in "surround sound" in order to infuse the workplace with offerings that promote and reward healthy choices.

By creating a seamless wellbeing experience, where every aspect of employees' health is addressed and easily accessible, you will be able to secure high levels of adoption, and thereby influence key outcomes such as performance, engagement, and the capacity to withstand stress. This requires a shift in thinking from health as something that is practiced annually at the doctor's office for a routine check-up, to something that is addressed on a day-to-day basis through lifestyle habits. Wellness initiatives must be designed to be less clinical and more lifestyle-oriented, with the intention of teaching employees how to maximize their energy and improve performance at work and in life.

Good nutrition is a priority. This is especially true at SDZG, where the majority of employees have physically demanding jobs. (Animal keepers, for example, are constantly carrying large feed bags, pushing full wheelbarrows, and walking up and down steep terrain.) Meals and refreshments served at SDZG meetings have shifted from refined, sugary foods to Zoo-branded packages of nuts and granola to help employees stay alert and focused. Instead of traditional pastries and doughnuts, employees are offered yogurt and healthy, low-fat muffins. Healthy food options are featured at guest food service outlets and in the employee cafeteria to boost energy and enhance performance. The menu at the Sabertooth Grill at Elephant Odyssey, for example, includes fresh ingredients from local farms and delicious dishes that support the local community and promote sustainability.

## ZOOView

*WellnessConnect* is an online portal where SDZG employees can join a group chat on wellbeing, access their Health Risk Assessment, connect with coworkers and exchange healthy recipes, participate in health challenges and events, and find self-help resources. Employees earn points for sending an e-motivational card, submitting a healthy success story, or collaborating with a "wellness buddy."

## The Seven Pillars of Wellbeing

When your life is balanced and you are thriving in all areas, you have the physical energy, emotional connectedness, mental focus, and spiritual inspiration to withstand disruption. To quote best-selling author Stephen R. Covey, "Your physical health affects your mental health; your spiritual strength affects your social and emotional strength. As you improve in one dimension, you increase your ability in other dimensions as well."

The Seven Pillars of Wellbeing, as seen in Figure 7.1, are interdependent. When one area of wellbeing is neglected, it tends to impact the others. Consider the effects of not eating well, getting enough sleep, and exercising regularly (physical wellbeing) on your feelings of self-worth, connection to your purpose and your ability to contribute value (emotional wellbeing). Similarly, money concerns

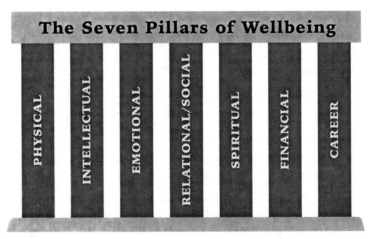

*Figure 7.1. The Seven Pillars of Wellbeing necessary for overall health.*

(financial wellbeing) can drain your energy and adversely affect your relationships at work and home (relational/social wellbeing).

## Physical Wellbeing

Physical health and wellbeing are the foundation of good health. As you improve your physical health, you naturally improve your mental and emotional health. Good physical health is a result of getting enough sleep, good nutrition, effective stress management, adequate hydration, avoidance of tobacco and drugs, regular exercise, and exposure to sunlight. As pressure rises and demands increase at work, there is tendency to sacrifice physical wellbeing in favor of compulsively long hours and tediously sedentary activities. (Some people consider sitting to be the new smoking.) A study in the *Annals of Internal Medicine* found that sedentary behavior increases our chances of illness that will kill us prematurely, even if we exercise.

Unfortunately, some companies still confuse lack of sleep and grabbing nutritionally deficient food on the go with high performance. Dr. Charles A. Czeisler, the Baldino professor of sleep medicine at Harvard Medical School, understands the physiological basis of the sleep imperative better than most. His message is simple: if you want to raise performance—both your own and your organization's—you need to get adequate sleep.

Sleep deficit and poor health habits are performance killers. In an effort to compensate for poor health habits induced by the frenetic pace of corporate life, some turn to sleep aids to shut down their overactive minds at the end of the day, reach for caffeine-laden drinks to stay awake, and choose sugary snacks for a short-term energy boost. The long-term effects of these poor habits lead to obesity, diabetes, risk for heart disease, increased health costs, and compromised productivity. Daily self-care habits that support you when you need it most are critical to building resilience.

## ZOOView

SDZG takes animal nutrition just as seriously as it does nutrition for employees. The Zoo's animal collection consumes a staggering amount of food each year: 31,200 pounds of apples; 16,800 pounds of bananas; 35,000 pounds of meat; 20,800 pounds of yams; 60,000 pounds of frozen fish; and 41,448 heads of lettuce.

SDZG employees receive a 20-percent discount on their insurance premiums by simply participating in the annual health risk assessment and annual biometric screening. Over 85 percent of employees take advantage of that perk.

## Intellectual Wellbeing

Cultivating intellectual wellbeing comes from engaging your organization in creative endeavors and stimulating learning to expand skills. When you seek to enhance creativity by exposing employees to different ideas, you harness their full potential. Reading books, participating in personal and professional development, and associating with big thinkers all cultivate intellectual wellbeing. As people develop intellectual curiosity and challenge their minds, they expand their ability to contribute and add value.

Each quarter, SDZG employees are invited to read a selected book that stimulates mental growth and stimulates the exploration of new ideas and understanding. Employees earn Roar Longer points for reading the book and answering some questions about it, and additional points for participating in a quarterly book club webinar/discussion. The books range from topics promoting financial wellness (Suze Orman's books have been popular!), to health/fitness/diet (e.g., *Born to Run, Get Some Headspace*, and *Fit at Last*), to motivational true stories (e.g., *Wild and Unbroken*) to animal-related fiction and non-fiction (e.g., *The Story of Edgar Sawtelle, H is for Hawk*, and *The Sixth Extinction*). This not only promotes "sharpening of one's saw," but also Rule #5 of the Rules of Engagement: taking time for recovery and renewal.

Learning labs make it easy for SDZG employees to submit innovative ideas to an online portal called Wild Ideas. They also can participate in My Academy, an online learning site that offers learning modules on a wide range of topics, from communication skills to animal care to various leadership classes and computer classes, as well as certification programs in areas like safety and animal husbandry. All courses are free and on demand.

Employees can voluntarily choose from an extensive list of course options, or managers can assign courses to employees through the Z-Max online performance management program.

## Emotional Wellbeing

Emotional wellbeing comes from recognizing your strengths and cultivating a strong sense of self-worth and confidence. To fully ground employees in the organization's values, vision, and mission, there must be alignment between individual values and those of the organization. This alignment provides a compelling reason for being, a passion and enthusiasm for the fulfillment of the organization's vision. When daily actions and behaviors are aligned with what is most important to the individual and the organization, employees have a clear sense of purpose and, ultimately, congruence, which leads to self-worth.

"The mission and values—our core tenets—establish the platform for those things we hold dear, the commitments that are most important for us to hang on to as we move toward the future, our vision," explains Beth Branning, corporate director of vision, innovation, and strategy. "SDZG's mission, to save species worldwide, is our compass," says Branning. "It's what will keep us focused on our vision.

We refer to our vision as 'The Call' because it's the call for every one of our employees to rally around the fight to save endangered species. No matter their title, responsibilities, or pay scale, every person who works for SDZG is united in focus and has a clear sense of purpose."

## Relational and Social Wellbeing

There is growing evidence demonstrating the link between relationships and wellbeing. Healthy relationships at work, home, and in the community positively impact physical, mental, and emotional health. They also help mitigate stress and promote longevity. The University of Minnesota reviewed 148 studies to find that those with strong relationships are 50 percent less likely to die prematurely.

Additionally, individuals with low social support were linked to health consequences including depression, decreased immune function, and higher blood pressure.

"Camaraderie is more than just having fun. It is also about creating a common sense of purpose and the mentality that we are in it together," wrote Christine Riordan in *Harvard Business Review.*

A sense of connection, support, and nurturing in the workplace can also contribute to higher engagement. Companies can develop social wellbeing through activities and events where employees socialize and volunteer during the workday to create social connections. Creating "social capital" around the water cooler and during lunch breaks, while fostering spontaneous interactions, is fast becoming an imperative for many companies. Relationships are a key engagement driver. Combined with networks in the workplace, they can make a good team great, and help keep a team together even when faced with disruptive events.

"The family-like work environment we have established at SDZG helps us to attract and retain the best talent," asserts president and

CEO Doug Myers. "If you speak to people who work or volunteer for San Diego Zoo Global, they never refer to it as a job and they never refer to it as a career. They'll always nod their head and say it's just a way of life. They integrate their work at SDZG with their personal life. When you meet their families, they feel the same way. They feel as if they're part of the San Diego Zoo Global family. It's as much about making your relationships at home work as it is making your relationships and your way of life at work be successful."

In fact, SDZG offers many family-oriented programs. Spouses and domestic partners of SDZG employees are given their own ID cards for free admission at all times to both the Zoo and the Safari Park. Children of SDZG employees are given free access to both at all times. Most children of Zoo employees participate in the very popular summer camp programs, at highly discounted prices. Many events happen throughout the year that families are invited to, culminating each December with the very popular Family Holiday Party at the Zoo.

## The Value of Volunteer Programs

SDZG's volunteer program, currently 1,700 strong, has events all year long to create bonding and a sense of family. At first glance, it may appear that these types of programs are merely "feel-good" activities with no real purpose, but recent studies have put that idea to rest and instead reveal a genuine business case for developing volunteer programs. Employers who establish formal volunteering programs for their employees benefit in several important and distinct ways. Current employees who volunteer through their workplace have a more positive feeling toward their employer and report a strengthened bond with coworkers, according to findings of a *UnitedHealthcare Survey* released in April 2010.

Since 1995, a program called Zoo Express has been bringing the Zoo—or at least a part of it—to people who are unable to get there.

Funded by donations, the program's focus is on children's hospitals, children with disabilities, and senior homes.

"For children and their parents dealing with health issues, friendly Zoo staff showing up with a small menagerie of animals is the perfect remedy," says Alison, a senior trainer and Zoo Express coordinator. "Zoo Express is one of the favorite parts of my job." This is an interactive program where people are encouraged to pet an animal and learn some fun facts about it. Animal ambassadors—Xena the sloth, Montana the singing dog, Jambo the (adorable) pygmy falcon, Armando Santiago the armadillo, and a multi-legged centipede—provide a welcome respite at hospitals and senior centers.

## Spiritual Wellbeing

Dr. Steven Southwick's book, *Resilience: The Science of Mastering Life's Greatest Challenges*, describes how some people overcome trauma caused by such events as abduction, war, and imprisonment by seeking comfort in spirituality or religion. Southwick offers examples of how spirituality helps people "meet the challenge and continue with purposeful lives…they bounce back and carry on."

There is a growing body of evidence indicating that spiritual practices are associated with improved health and wellbeing. Attending church or being part of a spiritual group can function as a source of social and emotional support, providing a sense of community, security, and belonging. In a study of spirituality in the workplace, MIT Sloane School of Management defines "spirituality" as "the basic feeling of being connected with one's complete self, others, and the entire universe." The study suggests that spirituality plays a vital role in people's lives by creating "interconnectedness." People who worked in organizations they perceived as "spiritual" also saw their organizations as "more profitable." They reported a freedom to bring more of their "complete selves" to work, and more fully express their creativity, emotions, and intelligence. In summary, organizations that were viewed as more spiritual tended to get more from employees.

## Financial Wellbeing

Do your employees feel on top of their finances and positive about the future, or are they feeling squeezed and struggling to make ends meet? Given that an estimated 70 percent of Americans live paycheck-to-paycheck, according to a survey released by Bankrate.com in 2012, companies that fail to support financial wellness may experience higher rates of absenteeism, increased health issues, and lost productivity. Conversely, employees who enjoy peace of mind regarding their personal finances are more inclined to be more engaged and productive.

While discussing personal finance has often been viewed as taboo in the workplace, a Barclays report confirms that 20 percent of U.K. employees think their financial situation affects their work, resulting in lost productivity that impacts the bottom line by 4 percent, and 38 percent said that they would move to a company that made financial wellbeing a priority.

Clearly, ignoring the importance of financial wellbeing can have adverse effects on organizational resilience, yet this often is overlooked. According to Healthways, only 15 percent of large U.S. companies offer financial education to employees.

Each year, as part of the monthly Roar Louder educational program for managers, there are always at least one or two financial education topics for the management team, which they are incentivized to attend. Employees are awarded financial wellness points by going on the Roar Longer wellness portal and reading articles about financial wellbeing, meeting quarterly with the retirement program providers, and attending the annual Retirement Fair.

## Roaring Ideas

Apple Inc. attracts employees with its "wellness center," a medical one-stop-shop, where they can get medical treatment, visit a nutritionist, chiropractor, or physical therapist for a nominal fee. Average wait time is less than five minutes. Inside the paperless, minimalistic exam rooms, there is a small table with an iPad and Mac (what else?). A coat closet for employees to store their belongings comes equipped with an iPhone charger.

## Career Wellbeing

If your employees don't enjoy their work, like one another, and have clear career paths, the odds of their doing well in the other pillars of wellbeing diminish. The influence of career wellbeing on overall wellbeing is often underestimated. People with high career wellbeing are more than twice as likely to be thriving in their lives overall.[2]

Fundamentally, every person needs to do something every day that is fulfilling. You can be financially secure (financial wellbeing), have good relationships (relational/social wellbeing), and be in good shape physically (physical wellbeing), yet if you don't like your work, you likely spend time worrying, complaining, and generally feeling unsatisfied. This causes stress, taking a toll on the other areas of your life.

When people show up to work excited, enthusiastic, and engaged, they are obviously more creative and productive, and more able to withstand pressure, "demandism," and adversity. In short, they are more resilient.

Tom Rath's *New York Times* bestseller, *Wellbeing: The Five Essential Elements*, considers career wellbeing to be the top consideration

---

[2] Wellbeing finder by Gallup

among all of the other varieties.[3] For example, according to Rath, wellbeing actually recovers more rapidly from the death of a spouse than it does from a sustained period of unemployment.

Career wellbeing is typically high for SDZG employees. When evaluating the employee value statement "Put Your Passion For Wildlife To Work," the SDZG HR team interviewed new hires and tenured employees, including those who recently left the organization, and found that they are proud of their work in conservation, as well as the Zoo's mission and vision. Safari Park HR director Laura Martella says, "People apply to work for SDZG because of what we do. And once hired they stay for a very long time."

### Roaring Ideas

Maine-based Idexx Laboratories provides a produce garden for its employees to tend. Many studies have shown gardening supports mental health. Don't have access to a garden patch? Research from Cornell University shows that adding indoor plants may boost attention and improve mood.[4] This is a highly cost-effective way to build resilience.

## Wellbeing as Company Culture

"Employees' perception of organizational support—the degree to which they believe your company cares about their wellbeing—determines the likelihood to which they participate in the program," says Aida Rosa, SDZG benefits director. "We try to remove any potential barriers to employees participating in our Roar Longer. To this end,

---

[3] *Wellbeing: The Five Essential Elements* will provide you with a holistic view of what contributes to your wellbeing over a lifetime. Tom Rath, James K. Harter, Gallup Press, 2010

[4] *Journal of Environmental Psychology*, Volume 31, Issue 1, March 2011, Pages 99–105 "Benefits of indoor plants on attention capacity in an office setting," Ruth K. Raanaasa, Katinka Horgen Evensena, Debra Richb, Gunn Sjøstrøma, and Grete Patila

we give employees ample opportunity, including paid time, to attend Roar Longer activities."

Wellbeing must be woven through the fabric of the organization so that employees have the freedom to improve theirs. If there are structural or cultural barriers, they will shrug it off. For example, if your company offers a health or fitness event, but department managers are reluctant to give employees time off from their duties, it's not going to go very far toward improving health.

Organizations that take a holistic view recognize that how they are known and their identity influences employees' commitment to wellbeing. "Roar Longer is a comprehensive approach that integrates wellbeing in the beliefs, behaviors, and systems at SDZG," says Rosa. "We expect leaders to create a work environment that supports wellbeing, and employees to take responsibility for their wellbeing. After all, one of our Rules of Engagement is 'Strive for Balance'."

## Zoo Print for Success

🐾 Evaluate your organization's approach to wellbeing. Is it a seamless and holistic experience?

🐾 Assess the impact of employee wellbeing on your organization's resiliency.

🐾 Identify ways in which you can integrate wellbeing into your corporate culture to improve overall quality of life and drive performance and productivity.

## World-Famous Leadership Questions

🐾 How effectively do you model the seven pillars of wellbeing for your team?

🐾 What commitments would you need to let go of, and what new commitments would you need to make, in order to achieve better wellbeing for yourself and your organization?

🐾 What one habit, structure, or process are you willing to change right now to improve wellbeing in your organization?

## ROAR LOUDER

Take a stand for wellbeing by demonstrating your commitment. Set aside one hour a day, every day, to "sharpen the saw"—improve your physical, intellectual, emotional, relational, spiritual, financial, or career wellbeing.

CHAPTER

# 8

# Encouraging Renewal

*Calmness is critical to being able to think clearly and deeply. Instead,*
*feeling stretched and stressed and pushed, we increasingly fuel ourselves*
*with adrenalin, noradrenalin, and cortisol. These fight or flight hormones*
*not only wreak havoc on our bodies, but also progressively shut down our*
*prefrontal cortex so we're more reactive, impulsive and focused on our*
*immediate survival rather than thinking long-term.*

– Tony Schwartz

When you are facing demands and pressures, the last thing you want to do is slow down and take a break. You might even be worried that if you do so you will lose your momentum and break your stride. More importantly, there seems to be a notion in the work world that taking time out for recovery and renewal is a sign of lack of ambition or laziness. Yet, the research suggests differently. Studies show that humans aren't designed for long periods of intense activity. Our ability to maintain focus and concentration for an extended time is limited. Although we don't readily recognize the signs of fatigue, they impact our ability to think clearly, maintain a calm focus, and control our emotions. The more fatigued we become, the more vulnerable we are to distractions and the less resilient we become.

In a normal workday, there is so much coming at you, so much to process. A 2010 LexisNexis survey of 1,700 white-collar workers in the United States, China, South Africa, the United Kingdom, and Australia revealed that on average employees spend more than half their workdays receiving and managing information rather than using it to do their jobs. Half of the surveyed workers also confessed that they were reaching a breaking point after which they would not be able to accommodate the deluge of data.[1] It's undeniable that we are bombarded with a never-ending stream of requests, deadlines, and imperatives, all of which are deemed to be important. Our brains are preoccupied with work most of the time. There is little "downtime."

What if the brain needs respite to remain productive and generate new ideas? "Idleness is not just a vacation, an indulgence or a vice; it is as indispensable to the brain as vitamin D is to the body, and deprived of it we suffer a mental affliction as disfiguring as rickets," essayist Tim Kreider wrote in *The New York Times*. "The space and quiet that idleness provides is a necessary condition for standing back from life and seeing it whole, for making unexpected connections and waiting for the wild summer lightning strikes of inspiration—it is, paradoxically, necessary to getting any work done."

## ZOOView

The Roar Longer six-week Relaxation Challenge encourages employees to stop and breathe, take stretch breaks, go for short walks, laugh, and use visualization to calm themselves.

## Short Sprints Work

Sporadic breaks and predictable time off for recovery renews energy, improves self-control, and helps to fuel performance. Time off can also help to stimulate creativity and heighten your aware-

---

[1] New Survey Reveals Extent, Impact of Information Overload on Workers; From Boston to Beijing, Professionals Feel Overwhelmed, Demoralized: U.S. Professionals, Like Peers Overseas, Struggle to Cope

Some Employers Taking Action but More Help is Needed, According to LexisNexis Workplace Productivity Survey. LexisNexis, October 2010

ness. Research on naps, meditation, nature walks, and the habits of exceptional artists and athletes reveals how mental breaks increase productivity, replenish attention, solidify memories, and encourage creativity.[2] Predictable time off is designated periods of time that employees are required to stop all work, unplug, and engage in activities that renew their energy. Although it seems counterintuitive, implementing a predictable time off approach actually increases efficiency and effectiveness. The payoff extends beyond the individual benefit to cultivate a work environment where employees are engaged, productive, and much more likely to stay.

Although the San Diego Zoo closes its gates to guests and turns down the lights at night, the Zoo and Safari Park never really close. Taking care of animals is a 24/7 endeavor. Zoo employees work hard, and their jobs can be unpredictable and demanding. SDZG leaders recognize employees must efficiently manage their energy with regular rest and recovery time.

This is clearly reinforced in the SDZG Rules of Engagement. Rule #3, Focus, states that "we stay 100 percent engaged at work." Rule #5, Strive for Balance, declares that "we are healthy, energized, and vital; we take time for recovery and renewal; we sharpen our saws—stay engaged at the top of our game!" Clearly, this part of the organization's Code of Conduct requires the support and modeling of its leaders.

## Promoting a Healthy Work-Life Balance

SDZG prides itself on being an organization in which employees should have every opportunity to have a healthy work/life balance. On the Roar Back Employee Satisfaction and Engagement Survey,

---

[2] Jabr, Ferris, "Why Your Brain Needs More Downtime: Research on naps, meditation, nature walks and the habits of exceptional artists and athletes reveals how mental breaks increase productivity, replenish attention, solidify memories and encourage creativity," *Scientific American*, October 2013

one of the highest scoring questions is: "My job allows me to effectively balance my work and personal life."

How does any organization ensure its employees are able to take time for recovery and renewal? There are many ways. For example, SDZG offers an abundant amount of annual leave (i.e., vacation) time to its employees, and wants them to take it! SDZG also has forged some great relationships with local wellness organizations to help with this, and regularly awards prizes at employee events for spa days, boot camps, and weekend getaways.

On a daily basis at SDZG, you will see groups of employees taking "walking breaks" around the perimeter of the Zoo—through Balboa Park, for example. Each step taken is automatically uploaded to the Roar Longer wellness portal, where progress is logged.

## Taking Back Your Lunch!

For most Americans, the lunch hour has become a hurried gobble of a quick sandwich while working. Research conducted by Right Management shows that only one in five people step away for a midday meal. The average worker takes less than 20 minutes away from his or her desk each day for lunch. Many never leave their desk at all and eat while catching up on email or hurrying to complete a task. Tony Schwartz, author of *The Way We're Working Isn't Working* and CEO of The Energy Project, wants to change that.

Schwartz, in an initiative called "Take Back Your Lunch," suggests workers ought to reclaim their midday break for the sake of health and sanity, not to mention their productivity. "The demand in people's lives overwhelms their capacity. We need to stop operating as if we were computers—we operate better when we pulse between spending and recovering energy," Schwartz says. A lunch break is not only important from a nutrition standpoint—to maintain stable blood sugar levels and renew energy, but it also gives your brain a chance to recuperate.

Short breaks sprinkled throughout the workday can allow workers to sit quietly, breathe deeply, connect with a friend or loved one, take a quick tour of the office to greet colleagues, walk up and down the stairs, stretch, drink a large glass of water, or have a healthy snack to renew energy and expand capacity. When these interludes are encouraged and scheduled at specific times, they provide much needed relief in typically overfull schedules.

For lunch breaks, SDZG hourly employees are required to take a full 30 minutes. In fact, the time clocks prohibit taking anything less! Meanwhile, researchers and conservationists at the SDZG Institute for Conservation Research enjoy a 3 p.m. dance party. Contrary to the academic environment, employees take turns in selecting their favorite dance tune, blast it through the intercom, and encourage coworkers to just not take themselves so seriously—all in the spirit of Rule of Engagement #6, Lighten Up.

## Roaring Ideas

Employees at The Energy Project use the "renewal" room to take a nap, meditate, or relax. A spacious lounge with free healthy snacks is a popular place for employees to hang out together. They are encouraged to take renewal breaks throughout the day, and to leave the office for lunch together. Workdays end at 6 p.m., and no one is expected to answer email in the evenings or on the weekends.

## Assessing the Cost of Stress

Workplace stress is a costly epidemic. According to statistics from the American Psychological Association (APA), a startling two-thirds of Americans say that work is a main source of stress in their lives. Approximately 30 percent of workers surveyed reported "extreme" stress levels.[3] While the physical effects of this epidemic are often emphasized, the economic consequences also are alarming. Workplace stress costs U.S. employers an estimated $200 billion to $300 billion per year in absenteeism, lower productivity, staff turnover, workers' compensation, medical insurance, and other stress-related expenses.[4] The problem is not limited to the United States. In fact, the United Nations' International Labor Organization defines occupational stress as a "global epidemic." Considering this, stress management may be business' most pressing challenge of the 21st century.

Experience tells us that certain factors such as a heavy workload, unclear job responsibilities, and job insecurity are stressors across organizations. Job stress can be reduced through thoughtful strategies that aren't necessarily costly or elaborate, such as through the many programs offered by SDZG's Roar Longer wellness program.

## Artistic Pursuits

Artistic pursuits also help reduce stress, and also boost creativity. They give people a brief break from the daily pressures, and remind them, if even for a moment, of a time or place that holds sweet memories. "We're a creative group over here, but we have tense, stressful deadlines. To balance our stress, we've painted a wall as a chalkboard that has worked wonders for all of us," SDZG marketing team members Melissa and Jenny report. "Employees are encouraged to add artwork to a creative theme that is changed every two weeks. It is morale building, a team endeavor, and the creative responses have been so rewarding. Located in the kitchen, employees stop by, stand and grin, and are often amazed at their coworker's talent and ability to shift stress into pleasure."

---

[3] American Psychological Association. "Stress Survey: Stress a Major Health Problem in the U.S." APA Help Center. 2007. "Stress in America." 7 Oct. 2008.

[4] American Institute of Stress. "Job Stress." Wein, Harrison, Ph.D. "Stress and Disease: New Perspectives."

## Exercise

Another stress reducer for SDZG employees is exercise. SDZG partnered with a popular local fitness trainer to deliver a daily 60-minute "boot camp" outside in Balboa Park. These are offered at a reduced price, for which SDZG subsidizes a portion, and a hefty amount of wellness points are offered as well. This program has been very popular: you can go by beautiful Balboa Park at either 6 a.m. or 6 p.m. on any day and see a random group of employees—staff and senior managers alike—having a great time working out together.

Flex time, work from home, and job sharing are becoming more common as a viable means to reduce work/life stress for workers. Comprehensive wellness programs, exercise breaks, walking meetings, yoga, and fitness classes all help to lower stress levels while refreshing employees and increasing productivity.

## The Wellness Dividend of Plants and Nature

Another inexpensive, yet effective, way to reduce stress in the workplace is exposure to plants and nature. Or, in the case of the Zoo or Safari Park, spending a little time with animals. Allison Alberts, chief conservation and research officer at SDZG's Institute for Conservation Research, appreciates the need for proactive stress management. "Working in a scientific environment, hunched over a computer or lab bench can be very stressful," says Alberts. "I encourage our researchers to take a moment to get out from behind their desks, and go outside. Of course, in this wonderful environment, you are surrounded by nature. If you're having a bad day, you walk past the gorilla enclosure, and pretty soon, you're going to be having a good day."

## Managing Stress with Mindfulness

Mindfulness training, as described in Chapter 4, is an effective stress management technique being used more widely in companies. Michael

Baime, M.D., director of the Penn Program for Stress Management in Philadelphia and a leading authority on mindfulness training, conducted a three-month, mindfulness-based work site program at the Philadelphia-based Scheie Eye Institute. After employees learned and practiced mindfulness techniques for a period of six weeks, their reported emotional exhaustion decreased from nearly 25 percent to almost 15 percent. At the end of the full three-month program, depression and fatigue were both reduced by nearly half. [5]

## Roaring Ideas

Code Lavender, developed by the Cleveland Clinic, is the alert Houston Methodist hospital physicians, nurses, and staff use when they need emotional or spiritual support. The alert summons a team of holistic nurses within 30 minutes of each call to provide Reiki, massage, healthy snacks, water, and lavender arm bands to remind individuals to take time to relax. The Holistic Services Team also offers spiritual support and counseling.

## Making the Workplace Fun

"Spending time on my farm with my horses and various critters keeps me centered, balanced, and happy," says Nikki, a Safari Park animal keeper. "I have learned over the years (having once been a workaholic) that spending time doing what makes my heart sing allows me to be the best I can be when I'm on the job."

When people are having fun at work and on their own time, they are more productive, better able to maintain composure in a crisis, and will serve customers better. The business case for fun is gaining support with convincing data from a decade of research by the

---

[5] Baime, Michael, M.D., "Penn Program for Stress Management." Complementary/Alternative Therapies at the University of Pennsylvania. 4.1. (Winter 2005)

Great Place to Work Institute. Data from the one-million-person research database reveals that "great" companies consistently earn significantly higher marks for "fun." According to the Great Place To Work Institute's Trust Index© Employee Survey, data shows that "This is a fun place to work" is the single most highly correlated statement to "Taking everything into account, I consider this a great place to work."

This finding doesn't necessarily mean that simply focusing on creating a fun place to work will build a great workplace. Fun is not a driver of great workplaces, but it's an important barometer. Having fun at work doesn't mean getting a cake and a keg, and forcing folks to party. Fun means taking a new way of looking at something old and stale, or something that must be done, and mixing it up in a way that enhances camaraderie, builds trust, and invites everyone to be their authentic selves.[6]

## The Amazing Race

SDZG's Amazing Race, an employee favorite, is a combination of physical exercise, mental stimulation, relationship building, and learning. The annual event helps to reduce stress and cultivate joy, not to mention being a lot of fun. The 2014 race kicked off in the Safari Park's Benbough Amphitheater with 82 teams of two employees each. It incorporated math challenges, such as counting the numbers of rows, shade structures, and other artistic touches in the structure. The competition then moved on to Samburu Playground, where 30 teams found hidden clues and then raced to the Great Rift Lift. From there, teams sprinted down to the Roar & Snore Campground where the race took on a new flavor. One team member had to race around the campground searching for three s'mores ingredients: marshmallows, graham crackers, and chocolate. Once all three ingredients were

---

[6] Caccamese, Leslie, *Five Ways to Have More Workplace Fun*, Great Place to Work Institute. May 2012.

found, that person had to make a s'more, have SDZG's renowned costume character and educator, Doctor Zoolittle, add some cooked bugs, and then eat the "treat." Other colorful challenges followed throughout the property. Employees who weren't able to participate viewed the 65-minute live broadcast in Hunte Pavilion—just like a full episode of "The Amazing Race" television series.

## Roaring Ideas

Daytime naps may boost performance. When night shift air traffic controllers were given 40 minutes to nap—and slept an average of 19 minutes—they performed much better on tests that measured vigilance and reaction time.

## Stimulating Creativity

On the surface, daydreaming or taking time to be still seems counterproductive, yet it's at the core of creativity, fertile ground for innovation. That's why some of the most innovative companies in the world give employees time and space to engage in creative activities. They encourage daydreaming. For example, 3M has a 15 percent program where every engineer has an hour a day to do whatever he or she wants. Some might work on a side project or use the time to engage in a hobby. Some of 3M's most successful products, including the famous Post-It note, have been a result of this initiative.

Surrounded by nature, and often performing solo, contemplative tasks, some employees at SDZG are fortunate to have quiet time, time to be still. That's where some of SDZG's most unique and creative exhibits have been born, and it's how the Zoo's employees continue to innovate and design attractions that keep visitors coming back.

## Wild Ideas

A few years back, SDZG brainstormed various ways to capture innovative ideas. Out of that innovation the "Wild Ideas" program was born. Wild Ideas is an online portal that can be accessed by employees at any of the many kiosks that now exist around the various campuses, or via their work computers over the organization's intranet ("The Insider") to give innovative suggestions for doing something different or better. These suggestions are vetted through a group that was formed by the organization's strategic plan. From this process, many exciting innovations have come to fruition, including different aesthetic features, premium product tours, and employee break area enhancements.

Another great way in which SDZG employees are encouraged to "innovate" is through the annual "Zooper Stars" program. This is similar to employee-of-the-month programs. The difference here is that in January of each year, all of the previous year's Zooper Star winners gather together to brainstorm and vote on how to spend $50,000 on areas that only benefit employees. From this program, many exciting new features and enhancements have taken shape—all adding to the organization's resilience.

In 2014, weather and other local factors were creating less than expected attendance. SDZG implemented the standard measures one would expect: a market analysis, expense reviews, and pricing evaluations. But the organization added one other element to the mix. At Doug Myers' direction, they assembled action teams at both the Zoo and Safari Park, composed of animal care, operations, and marketing employees. These workers were asked to come together to identify potential new on-site revenue generators.

Within a few weeks, a number of innovations were implemented. These included reworking behind-the-scene tours, developing a new

"Early Morning with Pandas Tour" and a new "Breakfast with Tigers" experience. These additions helped supplement on-site revenues, and both facilities exceeded budgeted goals by the end of the year. The biggest benefit for the employees was the new relationships forged between the action team members, and the empowerment that each member felt.

## Stillness Brings Answers

We live in a loud world. Noise overtakes our lives, draining us mentally, emotionally, and spiritually. Renewal can be as simple as sitting in silence for a few minutes.

Stillness is a powerful way to build resilience. It allows us a pause, to calibrate with what matters most, and realign with our core values and desires. Stillness is where great ideas are seeded. The busier people are, the more important it is for them to set aside time every day to sit still. If you're an engineer and you're trying to solve a difficult problem, seated at your computer for hours, fixated on the solution, you might be better served to step away from your desk. Place yourself in a different environment, relax, be quiet, and the answer will probably emerge. You can't listen for the future when you are buried in present to-dos.

The first chapter in Martha Beck's book, *The Joy Diet: 10 Daily Practices for a Happier Life*,[7] is titled "Nothing." Beck's premise is that "doing nothing is the most productive activity you will ever undertake." Doing nothing for a few minutes can lead to unexpected joy, creativity, and greater capacity to deal with adversity, and enhanced resilience for the organization.

## Zoo Print for Success

&#x2766; Determine what your organization's culture is regarding work

---

[7] Beck, Martha, *The Joy Diet: 10 Daily Practices for a Happier Life*, Harmony, 2003

hours, time off, and the importance of managing stress.

❧ Identify how this culture is affecting employee wellbeing, engagement, and productivity, and if it is building resilience.

❧ Explore ways in which adequate recovery and renewal can be included, encouraged, and rewarded.

## World-Famous Leadership Questions

❧ Do you have adequate time off to stimulate creativity and heighten your awareness?

❧ How is stress affecting you? How is this either building or eroding your resilience? What are you willing to do about it?

## ROAR LOUDER

If you were to make a commitment to cultivating extraordinary creativity and fostering unexpected innovation in your organization, what new rituals, processes, and practices would you implement? How would this contribute to increased resilience?

CHAPTER
# 9

# Taking Control of Your Time and Energy

*Control your environment or it will control you.*

– Dan Ariel

If there is a single diagnostic indicator of a resilient organization, it may be how the work environment is organized to make the best use of time and energy. Distraction, fatigue, and excessive work demands undermine attention. To be truly productive, you need a balance of quiet, concentrated work time and social interactions—for example, meetings, collaboration, and downtime—where your valued team members can develop relationships.

As leaders face rising demands and feel constant pressure to get more done, they split their attention and sacrifice focus, reflection, creativity, and the ability to see the big picture. When they juggle multiple activities in an attempt to keep up, they become partially engaged in many things, but rarely fully engaged in anything. The result is perpetual frustration and a sense of hopelessness that can lead to burnout.

Most companies have elaborate procedures for justifying and managing expenditures. In contrast, time goes largely unmanaged. The never-ending stream of phone calls, emails, instant messages, meetings, and teleconferences consume hours in every worker's day. However, few companies have implemented rules to manage time and attention, and that takes a significant toll on people and productivity.

Without such time-managing measures, organizations become slow and bureaucratic, detracting from the accomplishment of key strategic goals. Employees become disgruntled and resentful that they have less time to spend with their families and communities. A resilient organization carefully manages its scarcest resources—time and energy—and implements strict guidelines to invest these wisely. Some have designated "quiet time" when interruptions are not allowed. Others have "quiet rooms," and some have agreed to use the tried and true method of posting a "do not disturb" sign on office doors, cubicles, or on the backs of chairs to take back control of attention. But that's only the beginning.

## ROARING IDEAS

The Boston Consulting Group implemented a modest innovation to improve quality of life. Designated team members were required to spend one weeknight out of the office and completely unplugged from work. The results were profound. Consultants on teams with mandatory time off had higher job satisfaction and a better work/life balance, and they felt they were learning more on the job.[1]

## Boosting Productivity

San Diego Zoo Global recognized the tendency of people to get caught up in the swirl of day-to-day demands, diminishing capacity to fulfill the big picture. As a result, it has implemented protocols to support employees in reducing distractions so they can get their work done safely and efficiently.

For example, SDZG encourages (and some departments require) all managers and lead employees to schedule full or half days where

---

[1] Perlow, Leslie A., *Sleeping with Your Smartphone: How to Break the 24/7 Habit and Change the Way You Work*, Harvard Business Review Press, May 2012

they focus 100 percent on achieving extraordinary productivity and results with meaningful projects rather than putting out fires and checking emails. HR managers are encouraged to use this time to plan, prepare, change the world, prevent crises, build relationships, renew their own energy levels, and really make great things happen— then share their extraordinary results and ideas with the rest of the HR management team. Many excellent programs have resulted from these efforts, such as the Roar Longer wellness program, the Roar Safer employee safety program, and most of the Zoo U leadership development offerings.

Additionally, SDZG managers were given cheat sheets, created by the HR department, on various email tricks and tools to assist with productivity. These include how to turn an email into an appointment, how to filter out emails, how to automatically move certain emails into set folders, and various other tasks that would have been more difficult to ascertain on one's own.

Andy Grove, the former CEO of Intel, once wrote, "Just as you would not permit a fellow employee to steal a piece of office equipment, so you shouldn't let anyone walk away with the time of his fellow managers." Of course, such thievery happens often unintentionally. Meetings creep onto the calendar with no clear plan or priority. Initiatives crop up, demanding management attention.[2] As a leader, it's your responsibility to help your team find balance between results and risk of burnout. To do this you have to sift through the chaos, reduce distractions, and establish structures and processes to help your team accomplish its most important goals.

## Establishing Positive Energy Habits

According to Tony Schwartz, CEO of the Energy Project and author of *The Way We're Working Isn't Working*, "Most large organizations

---

[2] Mankins, Michael C., Brahm, Chris, and Caimi, Gregory, "Your Scarcest Resource," *Harvard Business Review*, May 2014

invest in developing employees' skills, knowledge, and competence. Very few help build and sustain their capacity—their energy—which is typically taken for granted."

Schwartz also states, "Establishing positive energy habits that are driven by deeply held values is the most powerful method to effectively manage energy." When you clearly define what is most important to you, then align your daily actions and behaviors with your topmost values, your calendar will reflect your priorities. Most organizations and their employees are working at such a frenetic pace that they rarely pause in order to ask themselves how they want to be known, what they stand for. As a result, they let external demands dictate their calendars.

If providing an exceptional customer experience is highly valued, then you will insist employees turn off all distractions and give their full and undivided attention to customers' needs. If protecting your team's time and energy is a priority, then you will encourage them to check and respond to emails only at designated times, rather than maintaining an addictive attachment to checking the inbox throughout the day. At several companies, including Sony Entertainment, senior leaders collectively agreed to stop checking email during meetings as a way to make the meetings more focused and efficient.

If accomplishing critical tasks is paramount, then you will permit no-meeting time periods first thing in the morning so employees can focus on getting things done when they are fresh and focused. If productivity is vital, you will insist people take intermittent breaks to renew their energy. If quality family time at the end of the day is important to your organizational culture, then you will encourage employees to not deal with business emails after hours, and implement policies to help ensure that happens.

To manage time and energy, your organization's leaders need to acknowledge the impact of routine behaviors and take responsibility for instilling positive habits that will help protect their employees' time and sustain energy to build resilience.

The bottom line: positive energy habits expand capacity to get more done with higher levels of engagement on a sustainable basis.

## ZOOView

At SDZG, many employees use their exercise-tracking devices to record steps, which then are automatically uploaded onto the Roar Longer wellness portal and converted to points for the Roar Longer Wellness Program. It's very easy to achieve at least 12,000 steps a day at the San Diego Zoo.

Rule #5 of SDGZ's Rules of Engagement is "Strive for Balance," which includes coming to work and remaining healthy, energized, and vital; taking time for recovery and renewal; and constantly sharpening one's saw—all in order to stay engaged and at the top of one's game. Granted, the employees of SDZG have a distinct advantage in this area since the Zoo is located adjacent to San Diego's beautiful Balboa Park. For many, meetings take place while walking around, as opposed to being stuck in one's office. There are some managers who require 1:1 meetings to be conducted on foot, walking around the grounds. Additionally, many of the behind-the-scenes break areas are located in serene locations, with quiet areas to watch animals—places where employees can silently rest and renew.

Regardless of your organization's surroundings, you should be able to find a nearby place of beauty and fresh air in order to follow this model—perhaps a riverfront, or even a pocket park in a large city. It's good to get out!

Time and energy are the fundamental currency of high performance. At the beginning of each day you are allotted a specific amount of each. How you invest that currency determines your results and level of satisfaction. Are you investing time and energy in urgent but not important tasks that don't contribute to your long-term success, or are you intentionally allocating your most precious resources to activities that have future value?

## Designating Time for What Matters

What's the first thing employees do when they wake up? Do they check text messages and emails that have flooded their inboxes overnight? Do they become immersed in responding to other people's requests and demands, setting off a series of activities unrelated to their primary goals? The first few hours of the morning are typically the most valuable time to accomplish important tasks, yet for many this period is consumed with those sorts of stop-gap activities. Designating a period of uninterrupted time to the most crucial tasks before checking email could be a high payoff decision.

When you accomplish an important task first thing in the morning, followed by a purposeful break, you inevitably have a greater sense of fulfillment. You feel better about yourself. You have greater capability to address demands throughout the day. Performing at a high level requires that you deliberately and consciously set aside time for tasks that are aligned with your purpose, and the purpose of your organization. Fail to do this and your life can be swept away by a sea of demands that are likely more urgent than important.

At SDZG, employees use the morning to focus on important tasks—which is vital, since once the gates open, if they aren't deliberate in their focus, they can get thrown into the craziness that ensues when thousands of visitors descend upon the grounds. It's that serene morning time when exhibits get cleaned, animals get moved, projects get done, and much planning is done—all before 8:30 a.m.! Tim uses the hours between 6 a.m. and 8 a.m. as "Tim Time." He's either walking the Zoo grounds, saying hello to employees, seeing the animals—or he's on lockdown mode in his office, and his staff know not to bother him. By 8 a.m., the door is flung open, the phone is un-forwarded, and it's back into firefighting mode.

In order to focus on the things that are most important to your business success, your employees must stop trying to "get it all done." Multitasking can be overrated, and often produces less. When calendars and to-do lists are organized in the traditional way, it typically intensifies stress. Think about the daily battles your employees face with tasks and obligations. They probably feel exhausted at the end of the day only to realize they still didn't complete their most important goals. It is important to be intentional about time and banish distractions. When you do, you give employees a sense of control, a sense of accomplishment, and ultimately cultivate resilience.

## Banishing Distractions

The world has its own agenda. Ads, tweets, Facebook posts, and billboards are vying for your attention. Pop-ups on internet sites encourage you to click. Alerts on your mobile device, incoming emails and text messages demand your attention. You are subject to a constant bombardment of suggestions, requests, and demands from your environment from the minute you wake up in the morning. Dan Ariely, professor of psychology and behavioral economics at Duke University says, "It's like we're surrounded by scheming thieves: thieves of our time, thieves of our attention, thieves of our productivity."

The work environment typically is not acting in favor of productivity and wellbeing either. Employees are subject to constant distractions. Take for example the insidious "cubicle fly-bys" where employees distract their colleagues as they walk by with a request. Or, the familiar "do you have a minute?" that becomes a lengthy conversation. The unrelenting volume of internal messages, texting, phone calls, meetings, and social interactions can rob employees of hours of their day. Because of that it's important to consciously arrange your work environment to be free of distraction.

A factor as simple as noise can have significant impact on a person's ability to perform. A study at an elementary school in New Haven, Connecticut, located next to a railroad line, measured the impact of noise on academic performance. Researchers noted that sixth graders on the railroad side of the school were found to be a full year behind their counterparts on the quieter side. When the city, prompted by this study, installed noise pads, researchers found this erased the difference. Students on both sides of the building performed at the same level. [3]

The ability to focus one's attention is key to success in any organization, but maintaining attention for extended periods of time can be challenging. Research shows that daily meditation over a period of three months can increase attention span,[4] which is why many organizations are turning to it.

Researchers at University of California at Santa Barbara asked 48 undergraduate students to take a mindfulness class that emphasized the physical posture and mental strategies of focused-attention meditation. They were required to integrate mindfulness into their daily activities, and to complete 10 minutes of daily meditation outside of class. These exercises required focused attention to some aspect of sensory experience. When these students took the GRE (Graduate Record Examinations; the standardized tests considered for graduate school application) before and after the two weeks of

---

[3] Mullainathan, Sendhil, Scarcity: *Why Having Too Little Means So Much*, Times Books, 2013

[4] MacLean, Katherine A., "Intensive Meditation Training Improves Perceptual Discrimination and Sustained Attention" from *Psychological Science*, Department of Psychiatry and Behavioral Sciences, Johns Hopkins University School of Medicine, Baltimore, Md., June 2010

class, the average verbal score increased from 460 to 520. Students also improved on tests of working memory and focus.[5]

## Roaring Ideas

A simple boundary can change behavior. When Google put M&Ms in containers instead of out in the open, people ate three million less of them in one month.

## Changing the Environment

Changing the work environment is the most effective way to cultivate resilience. Altering how desks are arranged, where computers are placed, and location of gathering places can influence workers' ability to focus and be productive. The environment influences how people behave, decisions they make, and how they interact with each other and customers.

Herman Miller, the office furniture designers and manufacturer, has studied the effect of office setups on creativity and productivity. They are so convinced the placement of desks, design of chairs, and workspace design has impact on the way people feel and work, that they hired phlebotomists to draw workers' blood to monitor neural activity and skin conductance levels to see how various settings impacted physiology. Researchers studied time-lapse footage of a workplace coffee bar to observe where people congregate. They stuck accelerometers to office chairs, and used video to observe interactions while an eavesdropper took note of conversation topics. What did they find? The better the workplace design, the better the social interactions that led to increased contentment at work.

---

[5] Mrazek, Michael D., et al, "Mindfulness Training Improves Working Memory Capacity and GRE Performance While Reducing Mind Wandering," University of California, Santa Barbara, 2012

In the SDZG marketing department, which includes the sales force, graphic designers, the web team, editors and writers, and public relations, management designed an open-flow workspace, similar to that found in a large advertising agency. The goal is to increase communication, keep creativity and innovation flowing, and encourage the sharing of ideas and banter. When quiet time or a meeting space is needed, there are many small offices that one can duck into to take a private call. In the break room, SDZG installed a giant chalk wall themed for different times of the year. Though this was a major change at first (everyone was used to typical cubicles or offices previously), the results have been exciting: the culture has shifted to more of a free-thinking, innovation-inspiring, "advertising agency" environment, with a constant free-flowing stream of communication and idea sharing.

In developed countries, people on average sit three to eight hours a day. It is proven that prolonged sitting can cause injury, heart disease, and fatigue. Sitting for extended time periods is linked with visual symptoms, high triglycerides, obesity, insulin resistance, cardiovascular disease, and cancer. It has also been shown to increase discomfort and decreasing productivity.

What's more, the causal chain from prolonged, immobile sitting to possible health risks exists even when one sits in a highly adjustable, ergonomically supportive work chair. If sitting all day poses such risks, some say the answer is to stand. That's why experts now recommend standing five to 20 minutes each hour.

### Roaring Ideas

Dan Ariely's Timeful app prompts users with suggestions for the best times to do things they say they want to accomplish. When users respond with feedback, the app "learns" when they do and don't like to tackle particular tasks—hopefully assisting people to better manage their time and get more done.

## Zoo Print for Success

✤ Determine the key "focus busters" in your organization. What distracts people and robs them of precious time and energy?

✤ Identify ways in which you can minimize distractions, interruptions, and other time and energy vampires to protect employees' attention and cultivate resilience.

✤ Experiment with "quiet zones," "quiet times," or "do not disturb hours" to boost employee productivity.

## World-Famous Leadership Questions

✤ When you look at your calendar, what do you notice about your priorities in life?

✤ What positive energy habits can you implement to maximize your time and energy, and build resilience?

✤ Which distractions, if banished, would allow you to be more focused on what really matters?

## ROAR LOUDER

If you were to rearrange your work environment to cultivate greater resilience, what would you change?

## PART FOUR:

# Reimagining Communications

The third competency in the Resilience at Work™ Model, Reimagining Communications, bolsters your capacity and the agreements you have in your team or organization to tell the truth, be transparent and vulnerable, and remain positive.

Beginning with your first smile, you have been in training as a communicator. Communication is the root of relationships and everything that stems from them. Then why is it that communication, or lack thereof, is often a source of conflict and the cause of undesirable results among individuals and in organizations?

Truthful, authentic communication creates community, understanding, and mutual values. This kind of communication creates an environment of trust and loyalty, which leads to fulfillment. It breeds positivity. In challenging times, however, communication breaks down, and is often replaced with criticism, complaint, and condemnation. In this kind of environment, tension rises and negativity sets in, causing withdrawal and disengagement.

A lack of candor impacts a company's ability to perform optimally. When employees are proactively supported in telling the truth without fear of repercussion, problems can be identified and addressed early on, and leaders have the information they need to make optimal decisions.

Organizations that promote a culture of transparency and truth telling are better equipped to attract and retain top talent. In fact, research shows that employees value honesty more than any other perks. A 15Five survey indicates that 85 percent of employees are unsatisfied with the quality of communication in their workplace. According to the findings from over 1,000 full-time U.S. employees, 81 percent would rather join a company that values "open communication" than one that offers perks such as top health plans, free food, and gym memberships.

Honesty is not only the best policy; it's the only way to build a resilient organization.

CHAPTER
# 10

# Looking Forward and to Both Sides

*The voyage of discovery is not in seeking new*
*landscapes but in having new eyes.*

– Marcel Proust

It's difficult to see things as they really are. In physiology, the blind spot is the gap in our field of vision that is a result of the human eye's architecture. The eagle, however, has an uncanny ability to see forward and both sides at the same time, seeing precise detail from a high altitude. Likewise, world-famous leaders develop awareness and sight lines that inform them at all times.

Blind spots can have unintended consequences. They limit your scope of awareness, corrupt decisions, and can create silos of different understandings within the same organization. As people rise in leadership, they often have the tendency to be "protected" from the truths, and to overlook or simply fail to notice signs of challenge or trouble.

Garry Ridge, president and CEO of the WD-40 Company, and co-author with Ken Blanchard of *Helping People Win at Work: A Business Philosophy Called "Don't Mark My Paper, Help Me Get An A"*[1] tells a story of how easy it is to ignore important signs. On an international trip, Garry found himself in a hotel with a free evening. A beer, a take-out dinner, and an evening watching TV was a welcome opportunity. Soon after settling in, however, he heard alarm bells sounding. As a frequent traveler, the bells didn't startle or worry him

---

[1] Blanchard, Ken, and Ridge, Garry, *Helping People Win at Work: A Business Philosophy Called "Don't Mark My Paper, Help Me Get an A"*, Pearson Prentice Hall; 2009

at all. The alarms kept ringing and Garry kept ignoring them. Eventually someone knocked on his door and insisted he evacuate.

Outside on a cold, rainy London evening in shorts, t-shirt, and slippers, he was irritated that he hadn't paid attention to the alarm and changed his clothing before evacuating. His relaxing evening had been spoiled. And yet, as great leaders do, he looked for the learning opportunity. Where else was he ignoring besides alarm bells?

Ridge invited the audience to consider the same question by drawing a line down a page, labeling one column "personal" and the other "professional," then, in each column, writing down all the areas where they were not paying attention, ignoring signs, or perhaps even disregarding alarm bells. He asked the audience to consider the cost of this inattention.

No one is immune to blind spots, yet leaders can be especially vulnerable. When you are in that position, others assume you have the answers, that you are able to offer the right solutions. For some leaders, the *need to be right* can take precedence over *doing the right thing*. The latter requires courage to solicit the help of others, and to create an environment of truth and transparency where people are willing to point out your weaknesses and illuminate your blind spots. It can be rare for people to overcome the fear of jeopardizing their job security or career advancement by speaking out. The result is that those blind spots expand as people around you withdraw into silence.

San Diego Zoo Global president and CEO Doug Myers and a core group of his leadership team are working actively to eliminate blind spots. One example is the new strategic plan they developed in 2014 to lead the fight against extinction. While the team knew the plan was on point with the organization's vision, they took the extra step of forming a "new perspective" group as a way to solicit feedback and illuminate things that they may have been missing. This group was comprised of employees who were several levels down in the organization, including newer hires who had not yet been fully immersed in the culture.

Rather than march the strategic plan out of the executive office with the expectation that every person will fall into line, Myers and his team invited criticism. They embraced suggestions for modifications, and as a result the strategic plan received overwhelming support.

## Seeking the Truth

World-famous leaders courageously seek out their blind spots, rewarding others for being honest in their feedback. They are proactive in seeking the truth, inviting criticism from all levels in the organization. Listening to criticism can be difficult, but even if you don't agree, it offers an opportunity to look inside yourself and explore where you can grow. How else will you identify weaknesses and areas of improvement? If you think you're right but don't get feedback from anyone, how do you know for sure what we're doing is right?

"If it was all Shangri-La and rainbows here, if everything was perfect and the world loved us, if we didn't have any challenges or nemesis, what would inspire us to get up and take action—to continue pursuing our vision, or even have the audacity to set such a bold vision as ending extinction?" says Ted Molter, chief marketing officer for SDZG.

World-famous leaders, like those at SDZG, greet judgment and criticism with grace. They value the message and the messenger. They place a higher value on truth than they do on their own ego. They admit mistakes easily and quickly. They say things like "I was wrong on that issue." Once they have been judged or criticized, they don't waste time with regrets; they redirect their energy into solutions. They take action to clean up what needs to be cleaned up rather than make excuses, pretend it never happened, get defensive, or punish the messenger.

Seeking the truth and requesting feedback are vital pathways SDZG uses to overcome blind spots and better serve its constituents. Every organization has things that may escape notice. Regular feedback from guests, employees, volunteers, and the conservation community are a mainstay for SDZG. As frontrunners in the zoological world, they receive a good amount of criticism, and they actually revel in it as confirmation they are breaking new frontiers.

Leaders at SDZG stay abreast of the events and dynamics swirling around them through a variety of mechanisms like the Roar Back annual employee survey, the Animal Welfare Panel, the Communications Action Group, mystery shoppers, and guest exit interviews.

## Measuring Communication

In 2015, SDZG's Roar Back survey garnered an astonishing 98 percent participation rate. That equates to several thousand employees. One area in particular where the organization has seen much success, from the first Roar Back survey in 2005 to the most recent in 2016, is in the area of communication. In 2005's first survey, some of the lowest scoring questions pertained to communication—specifically that which flows from SDZG's executive team. The survey statement, "The executive team listens and responds to the ideas, opinions, and suggestions of SDZG employees," was the single lowest score, with a 47 percent satisfaction rate. Another survey statement, "The executive team communicates well with the rest of SDZG," scored 52 percent. "Information and knowledge are shared openly within SDZG" scored a paltry 48 percent.

This was a real wake-up call for SDZG's executive team. It strategically "raised the bar" on transparency in its communications. Executives worked to enhance their effective communication of SDZG's mission, vision, and strategy. They spent a lot of time visiting departments and talking to employees, and consciously made an effort to be more visible, more communicative, and to overall up their game in terms of leadership. The work paid off: the scoring on these questions has enjoyed large increases, and in 2015 each received their highest scores yet.

## Animal Welfare Panel

As described in a previous chapter, SDZG's Animal Welfare Panel invites reports from passionate employees. SDZG's employees are invested in the organization's mission and animal care overall. This process has proven to be an invaluable tool to deal with any suggestions, no matter how minor or major, regarding animal husbandry. The ideas can be anonymous or transparent. Either way, each suggestion immediately goes to a panel of experts, who do a full assessment. It has become not only a best practice for SDZG, but one now being modeled by zoos and aquariums nationwide.

## Communications Action Group

The Communications Action Group is comprised of representatives from every area of the Zoo and the Safari Park, as well as the Institute. Tim, CEO Doug Myers, and Becky Lynn, director of employee communication, moderate the group. They all meet prior to each open forum. The group brings questions, concerns, and suggestions they're hearing from their colleagues out into the open so that Myers can address them. The group's meetings have proven to be an accurate harbinger of concerns from within the organization, and also have motivated its members to step up and be the voice of their departments. Both Tim and Myers enjoy these meetings; they not only participate and learn, but also use the forum to help regularly update SDZG's strategic plan, mission, and vision.

## Guest Feedback

Director of performance improvement Adam Ringler manages guest feedback mechanisms. These include automated exit interviews and mystery-shopper programs administered by third-party providers. Kiosks with monitors and touch screens in English and Spanish are found at guest exits, gathering guest feedback on service, cleanliness, courtesy, food services, tours and attractions, as well as educational and entertainment experience. Monthly Guest Intelligence reports are reviewed thoroughly and distributed to department managers.

"Department managers receive reports on where they are doing well, and opportunities for improvement with specific suggestions," says Ringler. "One of the ratings we are consistently pleased with is how guests rate their knowledge of animal habitat and views on wildlife before and after their visit. On average, these scores increase two or more points annually, which validates how well our employees have imparted knowledge." The category "Courtesy of Staff and Volunteers" often rates as high as 9.62 out of 10 points.

Trained, third-party mystery shoppers visit the Zoo and Safari Park throughout year, with greater frequency in peak season. They rate all aspects of their experience according to specific guidelines, including how easy it is to seek out information on the SDZG website, call center guest service, information about premium events, quality of turnstile greeting, food service quality, park cleanliness, and overall guest experience. Special observations, such as employees chewing gum or wearing uniforms improperly, are solicited, and are of particular importance to maintain standards.

### ZOOView

Mystery shoppers rate SDZG animal encounter presentations on the delivery of three key messages:

1. SDZG is leading the fight against species extinction.
2. Wildlife is in danger, and with your support we can save species for many generations.
3. You can be a hero for wildlife by helping to support the program.

## Nurturing Truth-Telling and Transparency

Of all the expectations people have of leaders, honesty is the most critical. Even a single misstep in honesty can be very difficult, and perhaps impossible, to overcome. No matter how effective, competent, and professional you are, you will never be perceived as credible if you are caught telling lies. Italian politician Antonio Gramsci once said, "Telling the truth is always revolutionary." Credible leaders not only tell the truth, they also promote honesty throughout the organization. They are zealous hunting dogs of truth, sniffing out misunderstandings before they happen, digging for dishonesty, and constantly looking for secrets. They openly communicate about every aspect of the business, hiding nothing.

"The communication channels, specifically the Executive Update monthly meeting, provides a forum for managers to hear what is going on in our organization," says Beth Branning, SDZG's corporate director of vision, innovation, and strategy. "Each month, the CFO presents financial results that previously had not been distributed widely. Doug Myers reviews the entire board agenda—the good, the bad, and the ugly. These two activities are the epitome of transparency."

Creating an honest work culture requires formal commitments and diligent, deliberate effort day after day. It begins with rigorous communication that keeps all constituents informed. "My philosophy is you cannot communicate too much," says Lynn. "Redundancy is good. Our audience ranges from business experts to scientists to high school kids. We have to keep that in mind as we build communication pieces so that we accommodate preferences and different levels of interest."

*ZooView* and *GRRREAT News* are regular employee communications that reiterate the message of conservation, acknowledge accomplishments, and provide relevant information regarding safety, wellness, GRRREEN initiatives, and HR updates.

*ZOONOOZ*, the quarterly membership magazine published by the SDZG marketing team, is sent to every employee's home. This allows them to read the same messages being communicated to members. Press releases are distributed to all employees as well. "We don't want the public to find out news about the Zoo before the employees do, so we provide the opportunity for employees to be the first to hear," says Lynn.

Employees, guests, and volunteers can all follow the SDZG Facebook page, Twitter, and Flickr. Real time access to photos, information, and alerts are available on mobile apps. In some exhibits, webcams offer unique views of animal enclosures. All of this comes with the intention of establishing a culture of truth-telling and transparency in everything SDZG does, including the design of animal exhibits.

## The Elephant Odyssey

Elephant Odyssey is a prime example of SDZG's commitment to transparency. The exhibit is turned inside out—the back of the house is the front of the house. Guests can see everything keepers do with the animals. Nothing is hidden. "When you approach business in this way, it takes the criticism out of it," says Chief Marketing Officer Ted Molter. "You can see everything." Keepers are right there next to the guests—engaging, making eye contact, and having conversations while taking care of the animals.

"This is how we create transparency," Molter continues. "We felt it was necessary to acknowledge the criticism from people who have concerns about animals in these kinds of environments. We want to show them that we take the welfare of these animals to the highest level possible. It's not just enough to say we take really good care of them. We have to demonstrate it."

## ZOOView

"What's What" is an ad hoc communication that wards off the rumor mill. Any time Dr. Allison Alberts, chief conservation and research officer at SDZG, hears of something that staff are wondering about or questioning, she sends an email to all staff addressing the issue head on.

## Develop the Skin of a Rhino

The great physician and humanitarian Albert Schweitzer was once asked, "What does it take to create a life worth leading?" His answer: "The skin of a rhino and the soul of an angel." What a rare yet essential combination! A thin skin leads to trouble in life. The thinner the dermis, the less we are able to talk straight, and handle self-doubt or criticism from others. Instead, we must develop the skin of a rhino— the capacity to withstand the arrows directed toward us—to bravely chart a new course and lead people forward. We must resolve to not take things personally, and assume full responsibility.

As a leader you will be judged and criticized. If you aren't, you're not doing your job. When you accept a leadership role, you voluntarily agree to be under a microscope. Since every decision you make affects others, everyone will have an opinion about your decisions.

"While I try to get as much input and buy-in on decisions as I can, I know that I'm not here to please everyone," says Dwight Scott,

Zoo director. "Sometimes you have to have a thick skin. People tease me around here. You can't just be a *kumbaya* guy all the time. You have to be able to take a hard line on issues and know where you will not compromise. For me, maintaining integrity is key."

One criticism that SDZG is faced with periodically is that the San Diego Zoo and Safari Park are the highest-priced in the country, but they also happen to be the most visited. "When someone buys a ticket, they're saying there is a value proposition. They think it's worthy of the support. We work hard not to disappoint people," Molter explains. "People are supporting our conservation work with their wallets, so to speak, and they're doing it in extraordinary numbers."

When SDZG or any organization is faced with criticism, it has the opportunity to get attention for important proof points. For example, when SDZG brought elephants to the United States from Swaziland in the early 2000s, it was the first time in 20 years elephants had been transported to the United States from Africa. "Without criticism from detractors, most people would have just thought that bringing elephants to the San Diego Zoo was a normal occurrence," explains Molter. "Criticism from those who believed the elephants would be better off dead than coming to the zoo precipitated an important opportunity to educate the public and gain support for conservation."

Conversely, when you resist criticism and take a defensive posture, it creates more skepticism. People want to know why you are working so hard to convince them. Instead, SDZG has chosen to stay as far ahead of criticism as it can. As Molter says, "We anticipate it coming and ask how we will tell our story before we're questioned."

## Zoo Print for Success

🐾 Assess the "honesty health" of your organization. How truthful are your employees? How informed are your leaders?

❖ Identify ways in which you can encourage more candid feed-back in your organization to cultivate greater resilience.

## World-Famous Leadership Questions

❖ What are you failing to notice?

❖ What are you ignoring or resisting that may cause you discomfort in the future?

❖ What may be preventing the people around you from telling you what you ought to know?

## ROAR LOUDER

How can you banish fear from your work environment to encourage honesty and truth-telling to cultivate resilience?

CHAPTER
# 11

# Having Courageous Conversations

*Our work, our relationships, and our lives succeed or fail*
*one conversation at a time. While no single conversation*
*is guaranteed to transform a company, a relationship, or a*
*life, any single conversation can.*

– Susan Scott, *Fierce Conversations: Achieving Success at Work*
*and in Life One Conversation at a Time*

A commitment to being overwhelmingly honest is the foundation of a resilient organization. Courageous conversations require a sincere commitment to do good. They also call for courage. Your willingness to speak out about issues that are causing concern, provoking frustration, compromising relationships, or undermining your organization's reputation is critical. The desire to preserve peace and harmony can often take precedence over having a courageous conversation. Yet speaking the truth with kindness and respect almost always matters more than preserving harmony. Avoiding the risk of awkwardness, tension, or retribution for addressing issues compromises productivity and limits opportunities. Candid conversation and empathetic listening forge strong relationships, trust, and loyalty.

In all aspects of its operations, it's critical that SDZG has courageous conversations. Its leaders encourage open and transparent dialogue with employees.

## Speaking Out

Telling hard truths is exceedingly important for SDZG's success. Animal care inspires much passion and debate. Whenever a beloved Zoo animal is in its final days, or passes away, the messaging to the public is crucial. The truth of the matter is that animals, like humans, age, contract illnesses, and die at some point. Being straightforward about this, or whatever hard truth your organization faces, is what is most important.

One recent example of this was with regard to Nola, who was one of the few remaining northern white rhinos in existence until she passed away at age 41 in November 2015. Residing at the San Diego Zoo Safari Park, she was the subject of much passionate dialogue and opinions surrounding the best way to care for her. This involved everything from scientific methods that are underway to save this amazing species from going extinct, to the best habitat in which Nola was able to spend her final days.

## Controversy and the Value of Transparency

The more you withhold information, the more you become trapped by it, losing time and energy trying to conceal things. In a world rich with opportunities for people to discuss work-related issues through social media, anything less than full transparency can be costly, contributing to a loss of morale and erosion of trust. SDZG learned this valuable lesson when it embarked on a rebranding of the Wild Animal Park in 2011.

When SDZG leaders were considering changing the name of the Wild Animal Park to the San Diego Zoo Safari Park, they mapped out a well-designed communications plan. In advance of the internal announcement, some employees unhappy with the change took their case to social media. A "Save the Wild Animal Park" Facebook page burgeoned and the media took advantage of the situation by stirring up controversy.

Recognizing the budding controversy regarding the name change, SDZG leaders decided to be proactive and turn the situation into a learning moment. "We missed the opportunity to communicate to employees as soon as we could have," says Ted Molter, chief marketing officer, "and accordingly, we learned why involving them early in the decision-making process is so important. We realized that through their protests, employees were telling us how much they cared about our organization. We knew this was a crucial opportunity to earn their trust and pick up where we should have been in the beginning. We recognized our mistake."

"Leaders worked to regain trust, and now employees at the Safari Park are some of the happiest folks at SDZG," says Laura Martella, park HR director. "They feel like they played a part in the success of the change. The new identity of the park truly belongs to them."

The name change is a highly visible sign in the rebranding initiative, but more importantly, it's a recognition of what everybody did to make a transition to a much more successful operation. "The transition of the Park was accomplished far more successfully than the 'external experts' predicted," says Molter. The successful transition was proof of SDZG's resilience—the willingness of SDZG's leaders to address issues head on, take risks, then rebound from difficult circumstances and achieve unexpected results.

Shortly thereafter, the rebranding was the focus of an annual gathering of the Zoo's biggest donors. About 800 people who had given $25,000 or more, or had included the Zoo in their wills, filled a ballroom at the Sheraton San Diego. "This was the first time that I was able to stand in front of people and tell them why we were rebranding," says SDZG President and CEO Doug Myers. "I got through my whole presentation. About half the group applauded, and the other half booed. I said 'We are going to do this. It's some-thing we feel strongly about, and it is going to work. I hope you would step forward and believe in your Zoo'."

An emphasis on premium experiences like caravan tours, the Flightline Safari zipline, and custom safari excursions—all sold at "booking stations"—transformed the visitor experience. "Sales dipped briefly at the beginning of the transition, but by the time we hit summer that first year, it was clear that it was turning," says Bob McClure, Park director. "Finances started to improve, and we were doing better than our budget projections." By 2012, the Safari Park realized its best financial year in history. Park management had projected it would lose about $1 million—less than it lost in each of the few last years. Instead, it was in the black by almost $2 million—proof that resilience pays off.

## Eliminating Silence and Telling Hard Truths

Leaders don't always face easy or pleasant choices. In the end, the choice to have a courageous conversation, to tell the truth, will garner respect. People respect courageous, decisive leaders who discuss the hard truths, gently. The more that you demonstrate the courage to discuss the truths, the more likely the people who work with and for you will follow your lead. The more you avoid the truth, the greater the price you are likely to pay in terms of cynicism, frustration, and wasted effort. Avoidance of the truth can even cost lives.

In 2014, car manufacturer Toyota agreed to pay a staggering $1.2 billion to avoid prosecution for covering up severe safety problems with "unintended acceleration," and continuing to make cars with parts the FBI said Toyota "knew were deadly." According to FBI assistant director George Venizelos, Toyota "put sales over safety and profit over principle." When media speculation arose that Toyota was hiding defects, the company emphatically denied the allegations, claiming that their cars were safe and reliable. The ultimate tragedy in hiding the truth cost them dearly.

Who can forget the collapse of Enron and WorldCom? When you look at organizations that have suffered from crises, you will find that their problems often resulted from "cultures of silence." According to VitalSmarts, a culture of silence is where people see the warning signs an impending disaster and yet choose to remain silent. They know that if something doesn't change, there will be serious consequences, but no one is willing to speak out. Or, in the event they do, those who hear their concerns choose to hide the issue.

The truth can hurt, but it inspires too. "People spend too much time calculating the risks that come with being honest, and too little time thinking about the rewards," says Brad Blanton, author and founder of the Radical Honesty Network.[1] Blanton suggests that "radical honesty is addictive. Once people discover the truth, they fall in love with it."

## Choosing Truth Even When It Hurts

Constructive conflict is a rich, complex experience that stimulates creative thinking and challenges us to grow, says Robert K. Cooper, author of *The Other 90%: How to Unlock Your Vast Untapped Potential for Leadership and Life.* Encouraging courageous truth-telling over harmony invites you and your employees to engage more deeply in what is most important, what matters most. Seeking a true way to solve a problem, face a challenge, or overcome an obstacle almost always enlivens, clarifies, and empowers people to accomplish more. Instead of dealing with disengagement, dissatisfaction, frustration, and resentment head on, do you tend to skirt the issue, avoid the decision, and continue on, or do you choose truth and transparency to build a resilient team?

[1] Blanton, Brad, *Radical Honesty: How to Transform Your Life by Telling the Truth*, Dell, 1996

Do you have the guts to let someone go, encourage them to take the next step or change their course, or do you simply give them other assignments to keep them out of the way?

## ZOOView

A "solution box" has replaced the customary "suggestion box" at the SDZG Institute for Conservation Research. Employees are encouraged to offer ideas for innovation and improvement with a clearly identified pathway.

Building an environment where you can constructively tell people why their work isn't meeting expectations, or what they need to improve, takes time. As coaching and mentoring become ingrained, a culture is created where performance improves, engagement deepens, and resilience strengthens.

Take, for example, how difficult it can be to encourage an employee to leave to find his or her passion elsewhere, and then assist that employee in launching an endeavor that will lead to greater satisfaction and fulfillment—both personal and professional.

Charles (not his real name) had been with SDZG for 20 to 30 years. He was thrilled that SDZG was intent on becoming a conservation organization, but had become disenchanted—impatient with the slowness of change. In his efforts to quicken progress, he often would run into brick walls. "Charles's morale was low and he was frustrated, especially since his own non-profit, conservation organization he was growing on the side was demonstrating progress," says his former manager.

The security of a regular paycheck, health insurance, and concerns that his non-profit wouldn't succeed kept Charles in his job. But, it was clear to his manager that his heart was in his own endeavor. She knew that she would need to have a courageous conversation, telling Charles that he had the talent and expertise to make it on his own, and that both he and SDZG would be better served by him resigning. In a show of support and gratitude for many years of service, SDZG assisted Charles in launching his new effort.

Initial resentment gave way to excitement as Charles embarked on his new adventure. His non-profit organization is thriving. Charles ultimately thanked his former manager for pushing him to do what was required. In trying to understand the best fit for Charles, SDZG had demonstrated both courage and compassion. Rather than kick him out, they were able to help him find the right path.

## Roaring Ideas

It's no secret that U.S. employees spend a large chunk of their workday gossiping. A 2015 Accountemps survey of 320 workers and CFOs in 20 metropolitan areas found that gossiping about colleagues was considered the most prevalent breach of workplace etiquette.

## Banning Gossip, Beginning with You

It seems harmless. Social chit-chat at the water cooler, between customer interactions or over lunch. Speculation about a person's career, someone's relationship with a coworker, or debate about an upcoming change. Is it light conversation or gossip? Is there a difference?

There is a difference and it can wreak havoc in your organization. Friendly conversation that is neutral can create valuable social capital—it enhances relationships and builds camaraderie. Gossip, on the other hand, is usually negative, inflammatory, and diminishes others. There is typically no goodwill in gossip.

Gossip can have adverse side effects on an organization. It strains relationships, erodes trust, and may cause conflict. When gossip is tolerated, people feel uncertain and suspicious. "Gossip can be toxic," says Dwight Scott, Zoo director. "One of the tenets of Rule of Engagement #1, 'Use your word wisely,' is to avoid gossip. When a leader talks about individuals who are not present, you undermine your credibility."

Scott has a rule that nobody is spoken of behind their back. He believes this helps to create an environment where direct reports feel safe. "I encourage others to speak about people like they're in the room," Scott says. "I think it's easy to slip into the habit of saying things about someone or their opinion when they're not present that is different than the way you would say it if they were there."

Scott believes that banning gossip builds trust. "It lets people know that when they're not able to make a meeting or they're not part of a discussion that you're still going to speak about them in the same manner." People are smart enough to know that if you're the type of leader who's going to complain about people when they're not in the room, then they're suspicious that you're going to do the same thing behind their back when they're not around."

## Zoo Print for Success

- ❧ Assess your organization's capacity to tell the truth. Is truth-telling encouraged and rewarded? Where is harmony being chosen over truth?

- ❧ Identify opportunities to uncover hidden truths that build resilience.

## World-Famous Leadership Questions

- 🐾 What courageous conversations have you been avoiding?

- 🐾 What will be the payoff for having these conversations?

- 🐾 What secrets are you harboring? If this information was "leaked," what impact will it have on your relationships and overall success of your team?

## ROAR LOUDER

What steps would you need to take to create a work environment where courageous conversations are embraced and gossip isn't tolerated?

CHAPTER

**12**

# Taking Responsibility for Your Wake

*Corporations rival governments in wealth, influence, and power … If a values-driven approach to business can begin to redirect this vast power toward more constructive ends than the simple accumulation of wealth, the human race and Planet Earth will have a fighting chance.*

– Ben Cohen, *Values-Driven Business: How to Change the World, Make Money, and Have Fun*

Everything each of us says and does leaves a wake. Positive or negative. Our individual wakes are often bigger than we realize. According to Susan Scott, in her book, *Fierce Conversations*, "an emotional wake is what others remember after you've gone. How they feel. The aftermath, aftertaste, or afterglow."

There are two types of organizational wakes. One is created from the way you interact with your employees. The other is external: the wake your organization creates in your community will impact the way you are perceived by the marketplace, directly impacting your bottom line. Just as you ought to be mindful of the wake internal to your organization, so should you consciously construct your external wake. The two are inextricably linked.

## Mindfully Considering Your Internal Wake

Whether deliberate or unintentional, a negative internal wake can be costly. Sometimes in the rush of day-to-day life and work, you might trip over conversations or make hasty decisions and leave people feeling hurt, rejected, or disappointed. Chapter 10 considered the importance of being more conscious about the impact your words have on others. Every conversation counts. Every action has an effect.

Some feel that if others are hurt by their communications or actions, it's not their problem. In a leadership role, the wake of your words and actions is amplified by your title and authority. The wake you leave as a leader and an organization affects your relationships with employees, customers, vendors, and shareholders. People are scrutinizing everything you do and say to determine whether they can trust you, and if they want to follow you. They are watching and listening at all times to understand how much you care, and what really matters to you. Are you a good citizen? Are you responsible? Do you act with integrity? Does your interest extend beyond attainment of corporate goals and bottom-line profitability? Ultimately, how your employees and stakeholders feel about you and your organization is your responsibility.

## Managing Your External Wake

Your organization's external wake often comes down to social responsibility. "We have to be mindful of each and every communication, every decision," says Ted Molter, SDZG chief marketing officer. "As a conservation leader, every action we take is scrutinized by our internal and external stakeholders. One poorly executed response can have significant impact on our reputation and brand equity."

To this end, communication is very carefully managed at SDZG. "Taking responsibility for our wake helps to build a reservoir of goodwill. In the event we make a mistake, we are more resilient in times of crisis," Molter explains. SDZG's commitment to corporate social responsibility reinforces its reputation as honest and trustworthy.

Being a good steward of the environment is imperative as a zoological facility. "SDZG is striving to be at the forefront of social responsibility and social change in the arena of environmental responsibility," says Molter. "We have to keep finding ways to use the opportunity we have as a well-visited, well-recognized zoo and brand to educate people and show them how to care for our future. If there's a wake to create, that's the one that we need to do."

One way SDZG has managed its social wake, communicating a message that supports resilience, has been by creating the Internal Conservation Committee (ICC), a thriving grass-roots group that has broad representation throughout SDZG. Over time, it has made huge strides in shifting the organization's processes, positions, and practices toward environmental sustainability. Some key areas of success have been in the areas of waste diversion, paperless initiatives, carbon-footprint reduction, and water conservation. It has also become a reliable internal source for information and awareness among employees and volunteers. What kind of message does that send? One that ensures that SDZG's wake is positive.

## Positive Messaging and the Bottom Line

Companies in all industries and of all sizes recognize that corporate social responsibility plays an important role in the success of their business. Having a good reputation as a good corporate citizen aids your recruitment efforts, communicates a positive message to the world. That in turn helps you retain top talent, create better relationships with stakeholders, and strengthen customer loyalty.

Given the fierce competition for talented employees and the growing commitment to corporate citizenship, there is increasing evidence that a company's corporate citizenship activities are a legitimate, compelling, and increasingly important way to engage and retrain top talent.[1] There is also confirmation that employees with

---

[1] Bhattacharya, C.B., Sen, Sankar and Korschun, Daniel, Using Corporate Social Responsibility to Win the War for Talent, *MIT Sloan Management Review*, 2008

favorable opinions of their organization's socially responsible activities are more engaged, confident, and likely to state an intention to stay a while.[2] Not surprisingly, some organizations are making a commitment to corporate citizenship as part of their strategy to increase employee engagement.

"Americans' appetite for corporate involvement in social and environmental issues is voracious," states the 2013 Cone Communications Social Impact Study. "Just 7 percent of the U.S. population believes corporations only need be concerned with their bottom-line," states the study. "More than 90 percent look to companies to support social or environmental causes in some capacity, and 88 percent are eager to hear from those companies about those efforts." When corporate citizenship is approached thoughtfully, transparently, and with good intention, that messaging helps companies achieve the "holy grail" of the triple bottom line—results that benefit people, increased profit, and planetary improvements.

## ROARING IDEAS

Ben & Jerry's uses only fair trade ingredients and has developed a dairy farm sustainability program in its home state of Vermont. Tom's Shoes, another notable example of a company with corporate social responsibility at its core, donates one pair of shoes to a child in need for every pair a customer purchases.

A report published by the Boston College Center for Corporate Citizenship confirms that successful companies are incorporating environmental, community, and governance strategies as key elements of their business plans. An analysis of corporate citizenship strategies, operational structures, and business practices of 231

---

[2] "The Kenexa Research Institute Finds that Corporate Responsibility and Environmentally Friendly Business Practices Return the Investment," Employee Insight Report, 2010

companies found that above-average industry performers are more likely to have a formal corporate citizenship department, a program led at the executive level, and higher budgets for corporate citizenship and charitable giving.[3]

"Organizations must choose between being just residents of the communities in which they operate and becoming involved citizens," says Doug Myers, SDZG president and CEO. "It's not reasonable to expect the San Diego community will continue to support us, unless we are community friendly. It's a win-win proposition. We do everything we can to be a good corporate citizen, and in return, the citizens of San Diego have helped us grow into a globally recognized conservation organization."

## ZOOView

The City of San Diego has recognized SDZG recycling efforts every year since 1996, awarding it the annual Waste Reduction and Recycling Award. According to the city, "Many businesses have shown that using resources wisely leads to greater efficiency and contributes to their bottom line. Business who take the initiative to develop waste reduction and recycling programs really help make a difference in the quality of San Diego's environment today and in the future." Through these efforts, SDZG has not only been invaluable in assisting the city in communicating the importance of recycling and composting, but has also made a major contribution by diverting 80 percent of the animal waste and green waste generated by the Zoo and the Safari Park.

Besides being a leader of good environmental citizenship, SDZG effectively manages its external wake through a robust community outreach program. Since 1995, Zoo Express has been bringing the

---

[3] Boston College, Center for Corporate Citizenship, Carroll School of Management

Zoo—or at least a part of it—to people who are unable to get to the park. Funded by donations, the program's focus is on children's hospitals, children with disabilities, senior homes, and a variety of other facilities within a 30-minute radius of the Zoo.

The pediatrics unit at Kaiser Hospital in San Diego is decorated in a colorful rainforest theme, and when Zoo Express arrives, the excitement is palpable. "It's a breath of fresh air when the Zoo comes," says Lisa Beltran, child life specialist at the hospital. "The partnership with the Zoo makes such an impact on patients and their families during a vulnerable time in their lives." Zoo Express staff takes the animals into each room for the kids and their family to see. Each presentation has a conservation message tucked inside that empowers all ages to help the planet.

Another recent success in SDZG's wake management is its Children's TV programming. San Diego Zoo Kids Channel is a closed-circuit television network that provides San Diego Zoo programs for kids to watch during hospital stays at children's hospitals and Ronald McDonald Houses. It includes animal stories, interviews with animal keepers, live feeds from animal cams, and special shows designed just for this channel. San Diego Zoo Kids Channel launched in seven locations in 2014, and is now on its way across the nation. Anecdotal research shows that kids feel better when they watch these animal programs. Helping kids feel better and go home sooner, plus inspiring the next generation of wildlife lovers, is what San Diego Zoo Kids is all about.

"We have always believed in the importance of putting people in touch with animals as a way to conserve species," says Myers. "What we have heard from medical care professionals is that animal interaction and animal stories can also help promote wellbeing. San Diego Zoo Global has a wealth of animal stories and, through the generosity of Denny Sanford, we are able to make these stories available to the families at Rady Children's Hospital."

The exclusive San Diego Zoo Kids Channel is currently expanding to many more children's hospitals across the nation.

## ZOOView

Retail departments at the Zoo and Park eliminated polystyrene (Styrofoam™) cups. These cups were replaced with a variety of products, including some compostable cups made from poly-lactic acid (PLA)—a plastic substitute made from fermented plant starch. When SDZG learned that PLA cups were unacceptable for the local landfills' composting process, it eliminated PLA cups, replacing them with cups made of a recyclable material—Polyethylene Terephthalate, PETE #1.

## Other Green Programs

Companies that are best at creating positive external wakes are including environmental initiatives as a key component of their social responsibility platform, as well as a means to attract and retain talent. Coca Cola, for example, focuses resources on water stewardship, sustainable packaging, energy management, and climate protection. Johnson & Johnson claims that in order to fulfill its purpose to "improve the health and wellbeing of families everywhere," it must protect the environments in which people work and live. The company believes a healthy planet and a healthy community go hand in hand.

Feeling "green around the gills" or "green with envy" is not a good thing. But when you work at SDZG, going green and getting greener are part and parcel of the mission and vision. SDZG is always looking to see what it can do better to walk the talk of conservation and inspire others to go just a little greener. By minimizing its carbon footprint and treading lighter on the Earth, the organization is helping conserve wildlife. "By changing our behaviors, we can help others do the same and make a big difference," says Deirdre, a SDZG education specialist.

Some changes are small, and reverberations will take time. Other changes are large scale and dramatic. All are helping to make the world a better, greener place. Here are a few of SDZG's earnest green efforts:

- **Waste Not, Want Not:** SDZG participated in a pilot program with the City of San Diego's Environmental Services to divert its pre-consumer food waste from its food prep areas for both humans and animals. The goal was to divert about 10 percent more of its total food waste.

- **Liquid Gold:** The Zoo's Rainwater Collection Systems were increased to seven tanks located on Zoo grounds, with the potential of capturing 25,000 gallons of water. The Safari Park has diverted over 93 percent of its waste stream; between the Zoo and the Safari Park, over 8,800 tons of herbivore manure is diverted each year!

- **Paper Trail:** In 2015, the Zoo and Safari Park used nearly 18 million feet of paper in its restrooms—enough to go from San Diego to Alaska and back. Its new air hand dryers are fiercely efficient, saving paper and using 80 percent less energy than traditional warm-air hand dryers. They generate 70 percent less emissions than the use of paper towels.

- **Smaller Footprint:** The Zoo hosts a Pit Stop for Bike to Work Day, a nationally recognized event celebrated annually on the third Friday in May. All Zoo employees who use any form of alternative transportation are invited to stop by the

Pit Stop. Internal Conservation Committee members are on hand to answer conservation questions, and educators with animal ambassadors spread the message of leaving a smaller wake by reducing $CO_2$ emissions.

❧ **Heroes for Wildlife:** The public, and SDZG employees, can help bring endangered species back from the brink of extinction worldwide just by turning one's passion into action. Under a recent program (currently inactive), Heroes for Wildlife, anyone can pick an activity, create a fundraising campaign, and ask friends, family, classmates, and coworkers to support them, all via the SDZG Wildlife Conservancy website. Examples of this include "I RUN for Wildlife," "I BAKE for Wildlife," "I PAINT for Wildlife," or any activity you want.

❧ **GRRREEN Work Program:** SDZG celebrates individual employee successes in the areas of conservation and recycling through its GRRREEN Work Program. Twice a year, SDZG's Internal Conservation Committee awards a "sustainable" prize at the Zooper Bowl events to an employee who exemplifies green practices at work.

## Taking Control of Your Story

If you want to build organizational resilience by deliberately shaping the impact you have on stakeholders, you must take control of your own story. Consistently, thoughtful architecture of your reputation begins with taking responsibility for how others perceive you. When the San Diego Zoo Institute for Conservation Research (ICR) developed its departmental strategic plan, there were concerns that traditional marketing and media outreach were not getting enough grassroots attention for the multitude of conservation initiatives being addressed. Most fundraising and publicity focused on programs with high-profile species, and other significant projects received less attention.

"We realized we had to change ourselves," says Dr. Allison Alberts, chief conservation and research officer. "We developed a new strategy as part of our departmental strategic plan to become the best story that San Diego Zoo Global has to tell." The Institute was intent on becoming the Zoo's most exciting fundraising opportunity. To accomplish this goal, ICR leaders made some significant changes. The first was to stage "outreach days," when staff from PR, marketing, development, education, and the volunteers are invited to an open house.

"We have dozens of guests attend the bi-annual outreach days," says Dr. Alberts. "Attendees tour the building, hear about timely projects in each of the labs, and learn about the exciting things we are working on." Instead of expecting PR and marketing to take the initiative, ICR began reaching out to them. "It was a fundamental shift from that downward spiral of blaming everyone else, pointing fingers, and feeling hopeless, to looking inward and asking, 'what can we do to tell our story in a compelling manner?'" Alberts believes the new mission and vision are validation of how well ICR succeeded in getting people excited about the conservation part of the organization.

## Zoo Print for Success

❧ Assess the effect your organization's wake has on stakeholders.

❧ Analyze how successful your corporate responsibility strategy is in engaging stakeholders and creating goodwill.

❧ Consider how your organization leaves a positive wake for the communities that matter.

❧ Identify ways in which you can enhance your corporate

responsibility efforts by aligning them with what matters most to stakeholders.

## World-Famous Leadership Questions

🐾 What will others remember after you've gone? What kind of wake are you leaving?

🐾 Are you a good corporate citizen? Are you responsible? Do you act with integrity?

🐾 Do people believe your interest extends beyond attainment of corporate goals and bottom-line profitability?

## ROAR LOUDER

How can you create maximum goodwill for your organization so that in times of crisis you are resilient?

PART FIVE:

# Renewing Connections

Your success is driven by your connection and coherence with personal and organizational values, a sense of purpose, feelings of belonging, and the support of those around you.

Connection is the essence of humanity. The stronger the connections, the healthier and happier you are. This includes your personal connection to the philosophy or religion that offers truth and certainty, as well as clarity and alignment with what you value most. It also requires that your values are in accordance with the values of your organization. A disconnect in any of these areas results in dissonance, frustration, and lack of fulfillment, all of which threaten your resilience.

Connection means exchange. Something is offered, received, and then offered back in return. If you want to build trust, sustain high levels of employee engagement, and retain your best workers, good relationships are imperative. No business can succeed without fostering healthy relationships.

Donald Clifton, the former educational psychologist who founded Gallup and developed the Gallup Q12 engagement survey, insisted on measuring workplace friendships for good reason: it's one of the strongest predictors of productivity. Studies show that employees with a best friend at work tend to be more focused, more passionate, and more loyal to their organization. They get sick less often, suffer fewer accidents, and change jobs less frequently. They even have more satisfied customers.

The difference between communication and connection is give and take, and the trust and respect that result from it. People who trust and respect each other work together as a team, share a common commitment, and learn from each other.

CHAPTER

**13**

# Connecting People to the Why

*He who has a why to live for can bear almost any how.*

– Friedrich Nietzsche

Baby Boomers, Gen Xers, and especially Millennials, who now make up more than 50 percent of the workforce, want a sense of purpose at work. It's clear that today's workforce is increasingly concerned with doing good. People are tired of just showing up every day to perform a job. They want fulfillment at home and at work. In his book, *Drive*[1], Daniel H. Pink suggests that we are in a time when individual desire to have a positive impact in the world often ranks higher than pay scale when selecting a job. Millennials, in particular, want to feel like their work has real purpose, and they want to be home for dinner.

These factors confirm that now more than ever, an organization's mission must extend beyond a self-serving goal to dominate an industry, generate breakthrough profits, or develop the next best widget. "Our mission describes the organization's purpose and the work that we do. It's what sets us apart," says SDZG President and CEO Doug Myers. "Our vision, the statement of our shared future, is big enough to inspire employees, donors, and volunteers to follow us."

Companies are expected to cast a vision for greater purpose that wins the hearts and minds of all stakeholders. Organizations that

---

[1] Pink, Daniel H., Drive: The Surprising Truth About What Motivates Us, Riverhead Books, 2011

want to prosper will need to focus more on meaning. You can do this through a compelling mission and vision—one that offers employees a sense of pride, satisfaction, and fulfillment; a sense that they are contributing to a better world.

The mission statement for San Diego Zoo Global states that it is "committed to saving species worldwide by uniting our expertise in animal care and conservation science with our dedication to inspiring passion for nature." These words permeate every aspect of the organization, from the executive team to the researchers working in the field, the tour guides sharing information with guests, the animal care workers, and everyone in between. It is SDZG's reason for being. This vision, which some might consider audacious, unites all stakeholders in a common goal. It provides a clear sense of purpose and meaning, aligning all constituents to the fulfillment of the cause.

SDZG continues to expand its role in conserving endangered species, with more than 140 field projects in 80 countries around the world. "Today we are facing an extinction crisis, with species disappearing every day," says Myers. "To combat this crisis we needed an audacious mission that focuses our efforts toward creating successful outcomes, even if we have to do it by saving one species at a time."

Audacious but not impossible, as previous successes indicate. SDZG has played a role in reintroducing more than 43 species back to their native habitat during its 100-year history. With an estimated 20,000 species near extinction, the health and welfare of the planet requires a great deal of cooperation, commitment, and financial support from both internal and external stakeholders. That means effectively connecting important colleagues and supporters to the "why"—an approach that can be put to good use in any organization seeking resilience.

---

### ZOOView

SDZG's mission: We are committed to saving species worldwide by uniting our expertise in animal care and conservation science with our dedication to inspiring passion for nature.

SDZG's vision: We will lead the fight against extinction.

Rallying Cry: END EXTINCTION!

How? One species at a time.

---

## Leveraging Adversity

"Adversity causes some men to break, others to break records," claims William A. Ward, one of American history's most notable purveyors of inspirational articles, poems, and meditations. Going through and overcoming adversity builds strength. It shapes people and organizations into who they are now, and who they will become in the future. Adversity gives you the experience, the confidence to overcome, and a new way to deal with circumstances. Accomplishments in business, life, school, and athletics are always that much more satisfying when they follow adversity or challenge. When you think about the greatest achievements in the business world, many have come through adversity. SDZG is no exception.

In the early 2000s, SDZG put to the test philosopher Friedrich Nietzsche's often quoted adage, "What does not destroy me, makes me stronger."

"It was a perfect storm," explains Beth Branning, corporate director of vision, innovation, and strategy. The economy was in a downturn, and as is often the case in trying times, there is a tendency for people to hide in their respective silos and avoid collaborating for fear of being edged out.

"People felt uncertain and afraid," Branning adds. "Collaboration slowed as people tried to protect their jobs." SDZG had a strategic plan, which was more of a written document that would be referred to from time to time. "It wasn't guiding anyone's actions," explains Branning. Without a common vision for the future, people were concerned.

Under the right conditions, and with artful leadership, adversity may foster resilience. Mark Seery, a researcher at the Department of Psychology at the University at Buffalo, who co-authored a study published in the *Journal of Personality* and *Social Psychology,* says, "Adversity can help people develop a "psychological immune system." Indeed, trying times spawned a significant breakthrough at SDZG. In light of the situation, Myers decided that the organization needed a vision for the future.

"It was the first time the organization had created a vision," says Branning. "It helped to focus everyone's intention. It gave us all a clear sense of purpose." Though there may not have been 100 percent consensus on that particular vision, all employees across the organization were able to see that by sharing it, they could make some compromises and come to a common agreement about where SDZG needed to head.

The human resources function was a big part of the vision. An entire section in the strategic plan called "Supporting Processes" outlined all the key HR changes that needed to take place for SDZG to become a vibrant, resilient organization. This was the impetus for the overhaul of all the people practices to become what now are regarded as world-class.

Clarity of vision automatically creates focus and alignment. It sharpens intention and provides a framework for effective use of time and energy—an organization's most precious resources.

"Ten years ago, if you looked at the executive team's goals and priorities, there was a list of 20 imperatives," says Molter. "Now, it's more like five. We are much more focused than we were in the past. We know where we're going as an organization, and as a result our employees are more focused."

## Roaring Ideas

There are many T-shirt companies in the world, but Life is Good's mission sets it apart—going beyond fun clothing to "spread the power of optimism." Uplifting T-shirt slogans such as "Seas The Day" and "Forecast: Mostly Sunny" bring a sense of joy to customers whose purchases help fund The Life is Good Kids Foundation.

## Connecting People to the Purpose

It's not enough just to have a clear purpose. People at every level of the organization must live and breathe its values, mission, and vision. After all, your vision and values are what you stand on, what guide your daily actions and behaviors, inform decisions, and ultimately determine what you focus on. They are the lighthouse that calls every person forward and calibrates each individual. That, in turn, determine the direction your organization takes. If people aren't playing by the same rules, behaving according to the same standards, and fully bought into what's important, then they begin to navigate in different directions, resulting in inconsistency and lack of alignment results.

According to Simon Sinek, author of *Start With Why*, your why is "the purpose, cause, or belief that inspires you to do what you do." Sinek argues that when you start with "why" in everything that you do, you inspire action in a way that "what" doesn't. The "what"—

information about what you do—engages your logical mind, whereas the "why" engages your emotions. It speaks to your heart.

Your employees are most likely less interested in revenue growth or bottom-line profits than they are in going home every day feeling fulfilled. When your organization's "why" is compelling, it becomes a driving force. It gets people out of bed in the morning with a sense of purpose and passion. It fuels performance and drives productivity. When employees' personal "why" is aligned with your organization's "why," people are on task, enthusiastic, and engaged. They are also more resilient.

Connecting people to the "why" of your organization is like locking together two pieces of Velcro®. When fully connected, the bond is strong. There is congruence and clarity. On the other hand, when an individual is disconnected from his or her personal "why," or the "why" of the organization, like two pieces of Velcro® detaching, the result is disengagement, loss of focus, and lower performance. Purpose hinges on five core beliefs shown in Figure 13.1. When any of these beliefs are compromised, it affects the strength of the connection.

## PURPOSE IS...

**1 BELIEF IN PRODUCT OR SERVICE:** I am proud of the product or service my organization offers. It's aligned with my core values. I believe it provides a meaningful contribution and serves the greater good.

**2 BELIEF IN COMPANY:** I am proud of what my company represents and how it does business. My personal values and purpose are aligned with that of the company to foster congruence and a sense of integrity that leads to fulfillment.

**3 BELIEF IN LEADERSHIP:** I trust and respect leaders to act with integrity, make the right decisions, and treat people with kindness and respect. I trust that I will be treated fairly and given the opportunity to realize my potential.

**4 BELIEF IN TEAM:** I believe my team will have my back, supporting and assisting me when necessary. I feel deeply connected to my team. We have a strong sense of collaboration and cooperation. We trust and respect each other.

**5 BELIEF IN SELF:** I believe I have the tools and skills to do my job well. I am given the right training and coaching support to accomplish my goals and advance my career. I have the confidence I will excel and be rewarded accordingly.

*Figure 13.1: The five core beliefs create purpose.*

## Energizing the Vision

In the past 5 to 10 years, strategic direction and collaboration at SDZG have improved dramatically. "The organization is moving in one direction, whereas in prior years, there were bursts of 'world-famous' activity coming from various areas," explains Myers. With the mantra of ending extinction, everybody knows their role and is aligned with the direction. Everybody in the organization understands that, whatever their job is, it contributes to conservation.

"Before, if you were in education, you might have been trying to develop a top-notch program. Animals were secondary because you were fighting for resources. Now every person works together toward the vision of ending extinction," adds Molter. SDZG leaders refer to this as "The Call." This is a powerful call to action for every person at every level in the organization to set aside personal or department agendas and work together.

## Internal and External Focus

Connecting people to the purpose at SDZG is divided into internal and external focus. Internal focus is on employees. External focus includes volunteers, trustees, and the public at large. A well-designed communication strategy ensures all stakeholders are consistently reminded of the reason SDZG exists.

"I align all of internal communications to the strategic plan and the fulfillment of our vision," says Becky Lynn, director of employee communication. "The contents of the strategic plan itself are one of the communication goals. So everything that we do, whether it is new employee orientation, customer service training, every publication and communication, revolves around reinforcing our mission and living our values."

Look at the front page of *ZOONOOZ*, the SDZG member publication, *ZooView*, the employee newsletter, or *Fresh Tracks* and *Daily*

*Flash* updates, the daily communication pieces sent out each day to all employees. In any of these publications you will find a story about saving endangered species.

"The vision statement is highlighted on every press release as a way to keep the public recognizing that it's the purpose that's driving every communication," says Molter. "For example, if you're reading a press release about a new baby elephant, it's framed in terms of conservation." Values, vision, mission, and strategy are woven throughout every communication.

Energizing the vision requires transparency and accessibility. In the past 5 to 10 years SDZG has opened up the communication channels to include each and every stakeholder in The Call.

"At all-staff meetings, Doug is about as transparent as he can be," says Paula Brock, CFO. "He lays out the direction of the organization and invites employees to come along on the journey. He is right out front of the charge, leading the way, passionately imploring employees to get on board," Brock explains. Myers, in his humble and down-to-earth way, is straightforward. He understands that those who aren't on board with the vision may want to find alternative employment.

At quarterly executive updates, Myers and Brock apprise supervisors of where things are in terms of strategy and reconnect them with the values, mission, and vision. Communication Action Group representatives bring questions from their department about the mission and vision and strategy. "Leaders help them interpret those so that they can take those back to their teams," explains Branning. To further strengthen the importance of connection to the vision, the strategic imperatives are integrated into the performance management programs and form the foundation for goal setting at all levels.

**ZOOView**

In 2015, the Association for Strategic Planning (ASP) awarded SDZG the Richard Goodman Strategic Planning Award, the organization's top honor for innovation and excellence in strategic planning. "The SDZG team approach to strategic planning is credited with helping the organization maintain its leadership role in animal care and conservation," said Bill Bigler, ASP president.

## Hearing the Call: A Reason for Being

Ending extinction is powerful because it's focused. To some it might sound overly ambitious, yet SDZG employees understand that the role they play in ending extinction is important. "We bring species back from the brink, like we did with condors and like we're trying to do with northern white rhinos," says Steisha Ponczoch, HR technology manager, who was very active in the creation of The Call, being a member of the "New Perspectives Group" of managers guiding its creation. Once species are pulled back from the brink of extinction, SDZG often partners with other groups that handle the international and political aspects to transition the species all the way back to non-endangered status.

The condor is a good example. Lead toxicity has been identified as a leading cause of death in California condors. Condors are scavengers, and find lead bullets in animal carcasses. These grand birds can inadvertently consume bullets, and the lead poisons them. "San Diego Zoo Global is not at its heart a political organization. We are scientists and conservationists—learning about and working to solve conservation problems," says Molter. "SDZG can identify what's impacting the condors, and help solve some of those problems at a grassroots level. We then work in partnership with other organizations and local communities to effect change."

"The focus of SDZG's mission is species on the brink," Molter continues. "This is where we rally all our stakeholders around the cause, create media exposure, and begin to turn things around."

## Three Strategic Priorities

The Call has replaced The Lynx, SDZG's original strategic plan, as the Zoo reaches its 100th birthday. Its purpose is to awaken the world to the plight of wildlife, and to provide hope for the future of nature. To lead the fight against extinction, SDZG's three new strategic priorities are crucial elements to bring the vision to life. They are:

1. UNITE internally and externally with a laser focus on our cause.

2. FIGHT against extinction of animal and plant species.

3. IGNITE a life-changing passion for wildlife.

For these three priorities, there are strategies that unite SDZG in building capacity and maximizing its resources—strategies to fight or pick battles, lead the charge, and sustain the momentum. And strategies to ignite passion, recruit champions, and inspire personal responsibility.

How will SDZG reach these aggressive goals? Who will do it? "It will take each and every one of us. From employees and volunteers on the grounds who inspire our guests' passion for nature; to those who speak in the community and at scientific gatherings sharing our conservation successes; to our collaborative partners in the field; and every employee," says Myers. "We can't fight extinction alone. We'll lead the fight in this crucial battle by saving species, but we'll need to partner with many other organizations, all joined in this common cause."

## Cultivating Purpose

Cultivating a strong sense of purpose in your organization is a key to driving performance and profitability. In addition to financial benefits to an organization, the emotional, psychological, and health benefits are noteworthy. People who live with purpose are able to find meaning in the life's circumstances. Andrew Zolli, author of *Resilience,* describes these people as being able to "cognitively reappraise situations and regulate emotions, turning life's proverbial lemons into lemonade."

Ed Diener's research on the science of wellbeing has found that people with a strong sense of purpose are better able to handle the ups and downs of life.[2] In other words, purpose can offer a psychological buffer against obstacles.

According to the Center for Spirituality and Healing at the University of Minnesota and the nearby Charlson Meadows Renewal Center, a sense of purpose can enhance your health in the following ways:

- **Live longer.** A 2009 study of over 73,000 Japanese men and women found that those who had "ikigai," a strong connection to their sense of purpose, tended to live longer than those who didn't. In his study of "blue zones" (communities in the world in which people are more likely to live past 100), Dan Buettner, author of *The Blue Zones: 9 Lessons for Living Longer From the People Who've Lived the Longest,* identified a strong sense of purpose as a key factor most centenarians share. In 2014, researchers found that "having a purpose in life appears to widely buffer against mortality risk across the adult years."[3]

[2] Diener, E. Fujita, F., Tay, L., Biswas-Diener, R. (2012). Purpose, mood, and pleasure in predicting satisfaction judgments. Social Indicators Research; 105(3), 333-341.

[3] Buettner, D. (2009, September). Dan Buettner: *How to live to be 100+* [video file]. Retrieved from http://www.ted.com/talks/dan_buettner_how_to_live_to_be_100.html.

❧ **Protect against heart disease.** A 2008 study found that a lower level of purpose in Japanese men was associated with earlier death and cardiovascular disease. Research showed that "purpose is a possible protective factor against near-future myocardial infarction among those with coronary heart disease."[4]

❧ **Improve relationships.** In 2009, Richard Leider, author of *The Power of Purpose: Find Meaning, Live Longer, Better* teamed up with Metlife to assess the purpose of over 1,000 adults. They found that those with a high sense of meaning in their lives spent more time and attention on their loved ones and communities. On the whole, people with purpose tend to be more engaged with their families, colleagues, and neighbors, enjoying more satisfying relationships.[5]

## ROARING IDEAS

Founded in 2007, Sweetgreen is a destination for delicious, organic foods. It also provides education to young kids on healthy eating, fitness, sustainability, and where food comes from. Their Sweetlife Music Festival attracts 20,000 health-minded people every year who come together to listen to music, eat healthy food, and give back to a cause—their Sweetgreen In Schools charity partner, FoodCorps.

## Building Resilience with Purpose

Research shows that having a purpose larger than self is a key to effectively overcoming adversity.[6] Purpose also helps you to avoid

---

[4] Koizumi, M., Ito, H., Kaneko, Y., Motohashi, Y. (2008). "Effect of having a sense of purpose in life on the risk of death from cardiovascular diseases." *Journal of Epidemiology*;18(5):191-6.

[5] MetLife Mature Market Institute. (2009). "Discovering what matters: balancing money, medicine, and meaning." Westport, CT: Leider, Richard.

[6] Russo, SJ, Murrough, JW, Han, MH, Charney, DS, and Nestler, EJ, "Neurobiology of Resilience." *Nature Neuroscience.* 2012 Nov; 15(11):1475-84.

becoming discouraged or overwhelmed when faced with a problem or hardship. It serves as a foundation for establishing priorities and decision. You are less affected by short-term setbacks and you can draw on your commitment to what really matters to sustain you during challenging times.

Resilient organizations clearly articulate their purpose, and all stakeholders understand the meaning and significance of the mission and vision, as opposed to a decorative display of hollow words displayed in the main lobby area. This purpose and meaning is expressed in the culture—the guiding behaviors installed in the organization, or, as some would say, what people do when the boss isn't around. It informs decisions, policies, and procedures. When the day-to-day actions and behaviors of people in the organization are aligned with the purpose, it results in a more focused and ethical organization that produces better results.

When purpose is personal, it builds engagement. It shapes a collective ambition and builds or strengthens the organizational glue.[7] According to Douglas Ready, MIT Sloan School of Management, and Emily Truelove, author of *Collective Genius: The Art and Practice of Leading Innovation*, organizational "glue" is what reminds people why they chose to work for you, why they strive to add value, and why they stay. It's a combination of a compelling vision that speaks to the hearts and minds of people that is integrated into goals, strategies, and leadership behaviors. It creates a unified culture that enables an organization to withstand adversity and rise above circumstances to thrive.

## Zoo Print for Success

❧ Evaluate the credibility of your vision, mission, and values.

---

[7] Ready, Douglas A., and Truelove, Emily, "The Power of Collective Ambition," *Harvard Business Review*, December 2011.

☙ Assess to what degree stakeholders are connected to your company's purpose.

☙ Identify ways to create greater alignment and connection with your mission, vision, and values.

## World-Famous Leadership Questions

☙ What is your personal "why"?

☙ To what degree is your personal "why" aligned with the "why" of your organization?

☙ Where are there opportunities for you to model your organization's values in a way that inspires others to rally around your firm's cause?

## ROAR LOUDER

How can you more deeply engage the hearts and minds of all stakeholders to rally around your organization's vision, thereby building resilience?

CHAPTER
**14**

# Putting People First So Profits Will Follow

*Trust men and they will be true to you; treat them greatly,*
*and they will show themselves great.*

—Ralph Waldo Emerson

Leadership doesn't require heroism or grandiose acts. The best way to win the hearts and minds of people is through simple acts of appreciation and kindness. Some of the best leaders are down-to-earth and honestly straightforward—doing the right things in the right way at the right time. They are people-centric, taking into consideration how every decision will impact trust and loyalty, drive engagement, and establish stronger connection. Putting people first is key to building a resilient organization.

Although San Diego Zoo Global's reputation for being "world famous" is based on its impressive collection of animals and plants, leaders at SDZG understand that its greatest asset is its people. In economic downturns, when many companies slash jobs to contain expenses and protect profitability, SDZG has historically avoided laying off workers. "We owe our success to the many talented individuals who have dedicated themselves to our mission. They deserve our respect and loyalty, just as we expect the same from them," says Doug Myers, president and CEO.

Rather than cutting jobs, Zoo leaders have worked together to contain expenses, knowing that the long-term benefits of ensuring job security far outweigh the short-term gains. As we have shown in other chapters, the Zoo has a broad range of programs that show appreciation and demonstrate the value it places on its people, including an array of uniquely branded programs to reward, incentivize, engage, and further the careers of employees.

## Making Others Successful

The success of your team or organization is never about you. It depends on how effective you are at bringing out the best in every person—how brilliantly you "mine the gold" in others. Acclaimed English maestro and leadership author Benjamin Zander puts it well when he suggests, "As leaders, we depend for our success on our ability to make others successful."[1]

The hallmark of a "world-famous" leader is to care more about your team than you do about yourself. When you lead from this point of view, you surrender your personal agenda and are able to be of service to your team—empowering your staff members to fulfill their greatest potential. When you suspend your ego, set aside your personal importance, and act with humility, you are able to serve others with a sense of dedication and purpose that builds an exemplary organization—not necessarily a perfect company, but one worthy of respect.

What could be more satisfying than dedicating yourself to inspiring greatness in others?

World-famous leaders are driven by an unrelenting commitment to serve others—to explore the best pathway to harnessing the full potential and tapping all the skill, creativity, and brilliance in each team member. This is their primary focus, their guiding objective and their number-one priority.

---

[1] Zander, Benjamin and Rosamund Stone, *Leadership: The Art of Possibility: Transforming Professional and Personal Life*, Harvard Business School Press, 2000

For example, consider the "Visit a Job" program at SDZG. Employees are encouraged to broaden their skillsets and discover hidden talents through in-house professional development opportunities. These opportunities could be in various locations around the organization. You may be lucky enough to spend time in the Applied Animal Ecology division, learning about animal husbandry, translocation, and radio-tracking techniques for tortoises, a field survey for western snowy plovers, or a ride along to the Sierra San Pedro condor release site to tag and track birds.

For employees working in retail, food services, or guest relations, these unique learning programs serve to deepen their appreciation of the Zoo's mission, while sparking a desire to harness more of their potential.

When funding for professional development was eliminated due to budget constraints, leaders at the San Diego Zoo Institute for Conservation Research developed an internal development program. Employees were invited to offer a class in an area of expertise. "The cost of this program was zero, yet the value provided was priceless," says Dr. Allison Alberts, chief conservation and research officer. "When funding for outside development was reinstated, the conservation team elected to keep the internal program. Researchers who previously had little visibility were able to share their knowledge and expertise with colleagues, and in so doing harness more of their potential while developing the team's skills."

The truth is that for companies to be profitable and grow, they must continually create new value. To create new value, you need people to invent and innovate new products and services—new ways of doing things. You create this environment by investing in your staff, relentlessly developing their skills and talents, and connecting them to the vision. Companies such as SDZG, Google, Southwest, and Costco are known for their learning and development programs, and their commitment to putting people first, knowing that profits will follow.

World-famous leaders consistently ask themselves questions like, "Who can I help grow and succeed? What else can I do to convey gratitude and appreciate, respect, and honor? Where are there opportunities to acknowledge and thank someone? Who is being left behind, and what needs to be done to ensure that person has an exceptional work experience? Where is my own ego getting in the way of someone else's future?"

Rule #4 of SDZG's Rules of Engagement[2] is "Mine the Gold." This establishes the mindset and expectation that everyone bring out the best of themselves and others. It's simple, but not easy. When we "mine the gold" in others, we focus on their strengths, supporting them in becoming all they want to and can be. In the words of the great philosopher, Goethe, "We relate to others from the point of view of unseen potential."

This consciousness provides a framework for leaders to constantly seek out opportunities to reinforce and reward desired behaviors. It encourages team members to stretch beyond their comfort zone. Leaders are dedicated to seeking and finding the good in each individual, and authentically acknowledging it in a meaningful way. "Mine the Gold" requires a commitment to serving your team and putting their success and wellbeing first.

## Putting People Before Profits

Most leaders will agree that people are the greatest asset to the organization, yet how many act congruently with this belief? World-famous leaders are unrelenting in their courage to put people

---

[2] SDZG's Rules of Engagement are based on the *Six Keys to Excellence featured in Excellence at Work: The Six Keys to Inspire Passion in the Workplace* by Sandy Asch, Worldat-Work Press, 2007

first, before profits. It's rare to come across a leadership team with conscious integrity, courageous authenticity, and compelling vision that inspires people to rise up and be their best—leaders who have the courage to lead with straightforwardness and caring. In a world that seems to suffer from a compassion crisis and empathy deficit, to lead with compassion and caring, and to put people first, requires courage.

Do you have the courage to put people first with the faith that positive business results will follow? Are you able to withstand the pressure to be flamboyant in your actions, and instead rely on your heartfelt values? And, do you have the courage to be truly authentic— open and honest in a way that allows people to be themselves fully and completely? At the end of the day, are you willing to forego the accomplishment of the task or goal in favor of character?

Many companies have mission statements hanging on the wall, espousing values that put people first, but if you ask employees, those values often are not exhibited in the company culture. Consulting firm Booze Allen Hamilton has stated, "Most 'people strategies' are platitudes. They look good in corporate or staff presentations or on managers' office walls, but they aren't really connected to the business. Most annual reports contain the boilerplate, 'People are our most important asset' or words to that effect. Yet few companies manage these critical assets to maximize their long-term return."[3]

Although the conversation about putting people first has been heard in boardrooms for decades, discussions still mostly focus on financial data and the need to be "practical" about people decisions. Conscious organizations value their people not out of altruism or fear of a backlash, but because it makes good business sense. A focus on people tends to spill over into how a company treats its customers.

---

[3] *Putting People First—It's Good Business*, Booz Allen Hamilton Inc., 1999

It's no accident that companies like San Diego Zoo Global, Google, Southwest, Costco, and others are not only great places to work, but also score high in customer satisfaction scores. Employees who feel cared about tend to care about others.

## ROARING IDEAS

Costco, the members-only wholesaler often held up as an example of decency and generosity in the big box sector, made the 2015 Best Places to Work in Retail list. Costco earned shopper goodwill and positive PR for its refusal to open on Thanksgiving Day to allow employees time off with their families.[4]

## Caring for Others

To be a "world-famous" institution, SDZG must offer customer service to match. Secret shoppers, guest exit interviews, and polls confirm that Zoo guests are delighted with their experience. Year after year, satisfaction scores continue to rise.

To assist employees in delivering on the promise, SDZG developed the GRRREAT! Customer Service program. The GRRR in GRRREAT! stands for: Greeting guests; Responding; Reacting accordingly; and Resolving the situation. This program, led by in-house "star" employees, is mandatory for all new hires. Current employees retake the program at least every two years.

Elephant keeper Robbie exemplifies GRRREAT! customer service. He is one of SDZG's Heroes for Wildlife, employees who have gone above and beyond the call of duty to advocate for animal preservation. Robbie gave Chris Christie, governor of New Jersey, a tour of the Elephant Care Center. In preparation for the tour, Robbie

---

[4] Glassdoor, Best Places to Work, 2015

did some research and found out that the New Jersey legislature had passed progressive legislation prohibiting the importing, selling, or purchasing of any ivory or rhino horn product, with strict penalties for those who do.

At the beginning of the tour, Robbie thanked Christie for his commitment to preserving wildlife. The governor responded by admitting the ivory bill was sitting on his desk waiting to be signed. After an excellent tour and meeting one of the Zoo's best ambassadors, African elephant Tembo, Governor Christie told Robbie he was all that much more motivated to sign the bill as soon as he got home. Three days later, he did just that.

In too many organizations, pressure from key stakeholders and visibility of bottom-line revenue often win out over caring for employees. Leaders unwittingly place priority on the result, gripping on to the tasks in order to ensure the accomplishment of goals. The pressure to meet deadlines, make the sales numbers, or deliver the project comes with a reward that can often be at the cost of the people involved.

How often have you pushed, pressured, cajoled, or even threatened consequences if business objectives are missed, and in so doing forced your team members to compromise their wellbeing and make unfortunate sacrifices? Have you or your team members missed a child's sports game or music performance, another important family event, or the chance to enjoy a vacation because you felt compelled to complete a project? Ultimately, these experiences bring about feelings of resentment, frustration, or regret that breed cynicism and resignation.

## Disengagement: The Enemy of Resilience

Cynicism and resignation inevitably lead to disengagement and low performance, which not only impact bottom-line profits, but may also affect global socio-economic factors. In the "State of the

American Workforce" report published in 2013 by Gallup, findings indicate that 70 percent of American workers are "not engaged" or "actively disengaged," emotionally disconnected from their workplaces and less likely to be productive. Gallup estimates that these actively disengaged employees cost the U.S. from $450 billion to $550 billion each year in lost productivity.

Worldwide, 13 percent of employees are engaged. This translates to 900 million workers who are disengaged and 340 million around the globe who are actively connected with their work. Gallup further suggests that disengaged employees are more likely to steal from their companies, negatively influence their coworkers, miss work days, and drive customers away.

The report states: "People spend a substantial part of their lives working. As a result, the quality of their workplace experience is inevitably reflected in the quality of their lives. Gallup's finding that the vast majority of employees worldwide report an overall negative experience at work—and just one in eight are fully involved in and enthusiastic about their jobs—is important when considering why the global recovery remains sluggish, while social unrest abounds in many countries."[5]

Disengagement is the No. 1 enemy of a resilient organization. The truth is that for any business to thrive in good times and especially in bad, it must continually create and deliver value. For that you need people who are inspired and motivated to not just perform the required tasks, but to go above and beyond the requirements of their job descriptions.

## Conveying Appreciation and Gratitude

While there are many factors that contribute to employee engagement, conveying appreciation and gratitude plays an important role.

---

[5] *State of the Global Workplace: Employee Engagement Insights for Business Leaders,* Gallup, 2013

It's easy to fall into the trap of believing that as a leader you must implement costly initiatives to engage your team and drive performance, when in fact, small acts that involve little or no expense are often the most effective.

At SDZG, resources for employee recognition initiatives are limited. The Zoo operates on a very tight budget with little wiggle room. This invites leaders to be more creative, thoughtful, and caring. When you have a generous budget, it's easy to take the path of least resistance and spend money on a program, incentive, or rewards to motivate performance. The true test of leadership is when you are forced to stretch your personal commitment and thoughtfulness to convey appreciation.

The human resources group at SDZG works in very close quarters. To be fair, their humble offices could easily be challenged by many of the Zoo's beautiful animal enclosures. Yet, quarterly team meetings are always special: a fun outing, a great lunch, beach activities, or a gathering on the patio of a chic cupcake store. These simple gestures create a sense of joy and engagement among those on the HR team. This sentiment extends to the way in which HR representatives care for the Zoo's employees. The environment in the HR offices is kind, helpful, and supportive. The HR team goes out of its way to serve employees and model the GRRREAT! Customer Service model.

In addition to supervisor-driven recognition, SDZG employees are encouraged to thank and recognize each other on a daily basis through a GRRREAT! Work ticket. They are issued a stack of tickets that may be replenished throughout the year. When someone catches a coworker doing something great for a guest, member, or colleague, he or she fills out a thank you ticket and presents it to the employee as a simple gesture of recognition. Tickets then may be dropped into GRRREAT! boxes placed at each time clock. These employees are recognized with a modest $25 gift card.

The Zoo works hard year-round to show appreciation with such programs as *Roaring Rewards,* a comprehensive rewards and recognition program; *Zooper Bowls,* annual recognition events where employees are honored for their efforts; and special previews and holiday events. In addition, the entire month of October is dedicated to employee appreciation.

At SDZG, thoughtfully designed efforts not only foster a culture in which employees feel valued for their contributions, but also promote the company's core values. The *Zooper Heroes* and *Zooper Stars* programs honor employees who exemplify and foster the Zoo's values, as shown in Figure 14.1.

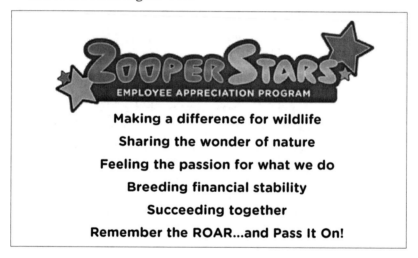

Figure 14.1. SDZG's values map to recognition programs such as Zooper Stars.

Clint, a *Zooper Hero,* works to make the Children's Zoo and Bird Show premier attractions. Clint helps breed financial stability for the Zoo by leading Animal Connections presentations, evening and Inside Look tours, special events and parties, donor tours, and public relations events. Clint's passion for "succeeding together" is demonstrated in his efforts to organize and run Front Plaza shows (the Front Plaza is the open area just inside of the entrance gates) to educate guests and connect them to wildlife. He also spearheaded the Zoo Express Program that visits 2000 children and adults at local Children's Hospitals and nursing homes annually.

## ZOOView

SDZG managers receive an annual budget to make purchases from the Zooper Market, an online company store where they can select Roaring Rewards and Zoo Perks—unique gifts and rewards for their team. The GRRREAT! Work Program offers on-the-spot recognition to employees. Outstanding employees are nominated by their peers for Zooper Hero and Zooper Star awards, all celebrated at the Zooper Bowl. The Zooper Troopers program recognizes years of service. And through the Roar Longer Wellness Program, employees earn bonus points for participation in wellness-related activities, such as the Roar Longer Book Club, in which they are encouraged to read health-related or inspirational books.

## ZOO Print for Success

❖ Assess how effectively people in your organization are acknowledged for their efforts.

❖ Develop a plan to convey appreciation to your team.

❖ Explore how you can bring your organization's vision, mission, and values more to life in your recognition programs.

## World-Famous Leadership Questions

❖ Are you making the interests of your team a priority?

❖ What else can you do to convey gratitude and appreciate, respect, and honor?

❖ What simple acts of caring are you overlooking?

❖ Where are there opportunities to acknowledge and thank someone personally for a job well done?

## ROAR LOUDER

If you're courageous, ask your team if they feel deeply valued and appreciated and how you could more effectively convey appreciation for their efforts.

CHAPTER
**15**

# Honoring the Greatness in Others

*Our chief want is someone who will inspire us to be what*
*we know we could be.*

– Ralph Waldo Emerson

In Eastern Tibet, people greet each other by saying, "Tashi deley," which means, "I honor the greatness in you. I honor the place in you where your courage, love, honor, hopes, and dreams live." Honoring the greatness in others begins with relating to people from the point of view of their unseen potential. Rather than judge or label a person's worth and capacity, you seek to bring out the best in them. You are relentless in your expectation, and request that they bring more of their creativity, skill, and brilliance to work every day.

This doesn't mean that you expect people to work unreasonably long hours or treat them unfairly. Instead, you are devoted to their success, knowing that the greatest fulfillment and satisfaction will come from their ability to fully express themselves and contribute at the highest level. You are unwilling to tolerate "status quo" and have the courage to hold "fierce," yet kind, conversations with anyone who is "coasting" or "checking out." Your unyielding intention is to ensure that every team member goes to sleep at night with a sense of pride and satisfaction. You want them to feel inspired because they contributed beyond their expectations and, in some cases, in ways they did not know were possible.

Much of San Diego Zoo Global's work is highly specialized. As a result, its leaders are constantly striving to ensure that everyone's talents are considered, and that they can successfully collaborate with others. SDZG's leaders realize the importance of honoring the greatness in every individual, while casting a wide net to include diverse skills and backgrounds.

SDZG creatively finds ways to bring in talented applicants, as well as "mining the gold" and finding their next leaders from within. Internally, SDZG has utilized several best-in-class programs to harness talent. For example, since many employees long to work directly with the animals in the collection, SDZG created the "Roar Corps." Forty entry-level employees were selected from various non-animal departments, regardless of previous animal experience or education, and placed into the program. These individuals are put on special assignments and "task forces" to work with the animals. The end goal is that they will be future animal keepers. There is rigorous classroom training on animal husbandry, and hands-on assignments throughout the year. The program is unique, to the extent that other zoos are now taking note and emulating similar internal development programs.

SDZG's "Zoo U College Relations Program" has become a fruitful way of finding talented superstars and future leaders. Prior to 2006, SDZG had no internship programs, no management training programs, and no college recruiting efforts whatsoever. When Tim was brought on board as chief human resources officer, he immediately saw this as a missed opportunity. Having been very involved in the college recruiting world while working for years in the hospitality industry, he recognized the perfect opportunity for college internships—not just in animal care, but in hospitality positions, customer service, marketing, information systems, research, and human resources.

Now SDZG travels to several college campuses each year, hiring interns to spend their summer working at the San Diego Zoo. This includes housing, mentoring, special projects, and assignments. Interns enjoy a fun schedule of social events and tourist opportunities, as well as a summer job. Many of the interns come several summers in a row, and many have also gone on to successful post-graduation careers within the organization.

In 2015, 140 college interns participated in SDZG's summer College Relations Program. Elijah was hired in the inaugural group of interns in 2006, working for two summers at the Safari Park, and one summer at the San Diego Zoo. When Elijah graduated from college, he was placed into a nine-month rotational management training program. Upon completion, he was promoted to operations supervisor at the Zoo, and is now a manager in the Safari Park's Safari Experiences Department. This is an excellent example of the beauty of programs designed to nurture development.

## Looking Beyond the Title

As Ralph Waldo Emerson said, "Treat a man as he is, and he will remain as he is. Treat a man as he could be, and he will become what he should be." When you hear someone's name or look at them, you can choose to see beneath and beyond their name, title, or history. Beneath judgments and assumptions there is a unique story—a life of love, loss, laughter, unfulfilled dreams, and hidden possibilities.

Honoring the greatness in others begins with a capacity to honor your own. When you are attuned to your own inherent potential, intentionally seeking to grow, you naturally see others in the same way. When you honor yourself, you are more likely to honor others. When you are engaged in continual learning to reach your next level of expression, you more adeptly encourage and inspire others to stretch beyond their limits. You ignite their passion and become an architect of the greatness that exists in others.

People will fall short. You will fall short of expectations from time to time. The natural tendency is to criticize and judge when you fail to achieve the desired outcome. It makes sense, then, that you will do the same when others fail to live up to your expectations. Repeated criticism and judgment establish a pattern of fear, resentment, and worry that erodes self-belief and ultimately affects the results people produce.

Criticism demoralizes, and can lead to defiance and withdrawal. It breeds resentment. A demoralized, resentful workforce lacks resilience—the energy and optimism to withstand disruption and thrive. Research at the University of Minnesota shows that negative events at work, such as being criticized, have a more powerful effect on an employee's mood than do positive events, such as receiving praise. The study reveals that employees react five times more strongly to a negative encounter with their boss than to a positive encounter.[1]

## ROARING IDEAS

The U.S. Bureau of Labor Statistics projects that by 2020, 50 percent of the workforce will be comprised of Millennials. Sometimes known as Generation Y, Millennials span the birth years 1980 to the early 2000s. This generation is the first to live and work online. Their strength is in multi-faceted communication, and interactive collaboration, which already is demanding a shift in the way leaders seek to bring out the best in their teams.

Business culture has long focused on weakness remediation, investing untold time and energy trying to address deficits, fill in gaps, and develop capabilities that are unnatural. However, while you

---

[1] Miner, Andrew G., Glomb, Theresa M., and Hulin, Charles, "Experience Sampling Mood and its Correlates at Work," Andrew G. Miner[1,†], Theresa M. Glomb[1,*] and Charles Hulin[2] *Journal of Occupational and Organizational Psychology*, Volume 78, Issue 2, pages 171–193, June 2005

are busy "fixing" yourself and others, you can overlook your greatest assets. Architects of greatness foster strengths rather than focus on weaknesses.

## Building Engagement

Honoring the greatness in others builds engagement. In 2007, the Gallup organization conducted a poll of more than 1,000 people, asking if they have the opportunity to do what they do best at work. Among those who disagreed or strongly disagreed with the statement, all reported being disengaged at their jobs. Other related Gallup studies have shown that people who are given the opportunity to focus on and utilize their strengths are six times more likely to be engaged.

One of the statements presented in the Roar Back! employee satisfaction survey mirrors one used by Gallup: "At work, I have the opportunity to do what I do best every day." The positive responses for this statement have risen annually. Participants also are asked to respond to the statement: "The management staff within my department encourages and supports my development." Positive responses to that one also continue to rise.

The positive trends reflected in these two statements can be attributed to SDZG's strategic push to increase engagement scores in the organization. Each department is required to produce a "Roar Back Action Plan," which describes what they will do differently in the coming year to raise the engagement scores.

## Getting Ego Out of the Way

Some leaders curtail the greatness of their teams. That's because they need to be the smartest person in the room. They dominate, and they stifle the creativity and flow of ideas. Consider leaders who diminish others by claiming their opinions aren't important, excluding them from important meetings and discussions. Leaders who believe they have all the answers fail to solicit opinions and insights that are potentially valuable. The result is underutilized talent, unrealized potential, and unharnessed creativity. As John Baldoni says, "Ego affirms a leader's ability to take charge. But checking the ego demonstrates a leader's ability to take charge of himself. That is critical to developing strong organizations which can achieve sustainable results."

Leaders who care less about asserting themselves, and who are more interested in building the social and intellectual capital in their organizations, suspend elitism and actively foster sharing of ideas. They believe that brilliance can be cultivated, and are willing to get their own egos out of the way to allow others to rise up, effectively harnessing the brainpower of the team. These leaders listen more than they talk. They ask good questions. They bring people together in an environment that unleashes their best ideas, and then step out the way.

When you create a culture of inviting people's ideas, engaging them to think in new ways, your team will contribute more, generating enhanced discretionary effort and more innovation—exactly what is needed for your organization's sustainable growth and success.

Dwight Scott, director of the San Diego Zoo, is a big proponent of "Mine the Gold," the fourth Rule of Engagement. "My role as a leader is to set everyone around me up for success," says Scott. "We have a lot of talented people in our organization, and sometimes, to be the best leader you just need to stay out of their way, deliver an inspiring vision, and then set them up for success."

Scott is typically the one in leadership meetings who refers to the Rules of Engagement. He reminds his colleagues of their imperative to bring out the best in each other and every situation.

## ROARING IDEAS

Ego can cost you your career as well as incur financial loss for your company. Chief executive of British Petroleum Tony Hayward's response to the impact of the oil spill in the Gulf of Mexico as "relatively tiny" compared with the "very big ocean" is associated with a $40 billion loss to BP.

## Bringing Out the Best

"Bringing out the best in others has been a focus for SDZG. This has been inspired and supported by the Rules of Engagement—particularly, Rule #4: Mine the Gold,"[2] agrees Doug Myers, president and CEO. "We have been on a steadfast mission to identify potential 'stars' on our bench. To this end we are always asking ourselves who are our next lead employees, supervisors, managers, directors, and executives."

The formal mid-year review discussion, including a career path component, helps to focus employees on what they want to do next, where their skills and talents can best be utilized As part of this process, each employee is asked what he or she wants to do next with their career. This then becomes a mandatory component of the formal mid-year review discussion, resulting in honest dialogue between managers and direct reports. Though turnover at SDZG is relatively low (for non-seasonal employees, it is about 5 percent annually), succession planning remains top of mind.

In 2015, every one of the 70 senior managers (including the executive leadership team) was asked point-blank who their future successors were in the organization, regardless of their potential retirement dates. Many surprises emerged from this question, and many of

[2] Mine the Gold is one of the Six Keys to Excellence and is used with permission of Alliance for Organizational Excellence LLC

those future successors were either enrolled in a robust Executive Leadership Development Program (a full 360-degree progress and individual development plan, executive coaching—individual and group—and high level in-class leadership programs), or they will be put in the program shortly. The point is, for SDZG, it's all about mining the gold—for future executives, leaders, supervisors, animal keepers, or other positions within the organization.

It seems to be working, based on the high level of internal promotions that happen for management positions. (The organization has made an oath to its employees that there would not be external hires for entry-level supervisory positions in most operations departments.) This also has contributed to the meteoric rise in the scores on this Roar Back statement: "We promote reliable, competent employees from within SDZG before looking outside." In fact, positive responses to this statement alone have jumped more than 20 percent as compared to 10 years ago, when there was no succession planning or Rules of Engagement in place.

## Identifying Stars

SDZG's internal management training programs are designed to identify "stars" and groom them for management.

Gail was hired as a food service clerk in 2000. She was nominated by her manager to participate in the Internal Operations Management Program in 2009 as a means to better utilize her skills and talents. She participated in a three-month rotational management training program at the San Diego Zoo Safari Park, with extraordinary success. This was the perfect example of an employee who had gone somewhat unnoticed for several years, then became a highly visible and respected contributor.

Upon graduation from the program, Gail was promoted to retail operations supervisor at the San Diego Zoo. A year later she was promoted to retail operations manager, and she is well on her way to moving up the ladder. "Every one of the 15 graduates of the Internal Operations Management Program have now been elevated from hourly jobs to management positions," says Adriana Martinez, HR director. A similar program was implemented in the animal care arena, to transition non-animal-care employees to animal keeper jobs, and keepers to animal care management.

## Diversity Drives Innovation

Stephen Covey once said, "Strength lies in differences, not in similarities." Diversity is critical for an organization's ability to innovate and adapt. Diversity of experiences, perspectives, cultures, genders, and age afford a company a richness of ideas and breed innovation. That, in turn, drives market growth. According to the Center for Talent Innovation, "When leaders embody diversity and their leadership culture embraces diversity, they create a "speak-up culture" that harnesses "point-of-pain" insights to meet the needs of underserved demographics—a dynamic that exerts a measurable impact on the bottom line."

There are two types of diversity. Gender and ethnicity, traits you are born with, represent *inherent* diversity. *Acquired* diversity includes traits that are gained from experience. For example, working with a predominantly female population can help you to develop an aptitude for gender differences. Living in a foreign country can develop your appreciation for cultural differences. A work environment brimming with both kinds of diversity stimulates "out of the box" ideas that can drive profitability. Employees of firms with 2-D diversity (inherent and acquired) are 45 percent more likely to report a growth in market share over the previous year and 70 percent more likely to report that the firm captured a new market.[3]

---

[3] Hewlett, Sylvia Ann, Marshall, Melinda, and Sherbin, Laura, "How Diversity Can Drive Innovation," *Harvard Business Review*, December 2013

McKinsey has been examining diversity in the workplace for several years. Its report, *Diversity Matters*, examined data sets for 366 public companies across a range of industries in Canada, Latin America, the United Kingdom, and the United States. The findings confirmed that "companies in the top quartile for racial and ethnic diversity are 35 percent more likely to have financial returns above their respective national industry medians."[4]

Many San Diego Zoo Global volunteer applicants have differing physical or cognitive abilities, and/or may experience a range within the spectrum of autism. Many individuals volunteer in specialized areas, such as the hummingbird aviary at the Zoo and the Petting Kraal at the Safari Park. Zoo and Safari Park guests have taken notice as well, and many have expressed admiration for the opportunities SDZG provides people of all abilities.

Most of us are attracted to certain types of individuals. Natural instinct draws us to people with whom we share similarities. When you cultivate an appreciation for people who look or act differently, and think in ways you don't, you open yourself to a wider pool of talent. Without exception, outstanding advancement and breakthrough results are a result of disparate ideas and talents brought together and harnessed in unusual ways.

## Diversity Fuels Resilience

Daniel Goleman, author of *Emotional Intelligence* and *Focus*, explains that diversity leads to greater productivity. According to Goleman, one of the most important reasons to value diversity in an organization is what he refers to as the "Group IQ." He calls it "the sum total of the best talent of every person on a team contributed with full force." A high-performing team typically displays a high group IQ. The best

---

[4] Hunt, Vivian, Layton, Dennis, and Prince, Sara, "New Research Makes It Increasingly Clear That Companies With More Diverse Workforces Perform Better Financially," McKinsey and Company, January 2015

predictors of success are most often how people on the team are valued, and the degree to which they embrace and harness differences.

Teams that leverage each person's strengths, that achieve a sense of harmony and collaboration while celebrating differences, exhibit the highest emotional intelligence. The more diverse teams with the larger array of talents and experiences will have the potential best performance. Research on high-performing teams conducted by Vanessa Druskat at the University of New Hampshire confirms a correlation between the collective emotional intelligence and a team's productivity,[5] and that makes for greater resilience.

## Zoo Print for Success

🐾 Identify how effectively you are utilizing all the talent, skill, and creativity available in your organization.

🐾 Assess the diversity of experiences, perspectives, cultures, genders, and age in your organization, and how you can embrace and embody the collective differences.

🐾 Develop a plan to reveal the greatness of every person and build resilience.

## World-Famous Leadership Questions

🐾 What greatness lies within each person on your team?

🐾 What steps will you take to unlock each and every person's potential, and fully harness all the skills and talents available in your team?

🐾 Where are there opportunities to infuse your organization with greater diversity to breed creativity and innovation?

---

[5] Druskat, V. U., & Wolff, S. B. (2001). "Group Emotional Competence and its Influence on Group Effectiveness." Cary Cherniss and Daniel Goleman (Eds.), *The Emotionally Intelligent Workplace* (pp. 132-155). San Francisco: Jossey-Bass.

## ROAR LOUDER

If you're courageous, ask a trusted colleague where your ego is getting in the way of someone's future. Then, take steps to get out of the way so that person can fulfill his her potential.

## PART SIX:

# Rebalancing Commitment

The last of the five Resilience at Work™ competencies is Rebalancing Commitments—your willingness to embrace change and adopt new habits that support and build resilience. It's your ability to persevere and prevail in any circumstances.

Commitment is emotional resolve, or a willingness to take on risk. It precedes action. It almost always requires courage. In this section you are invited to answer the question, how will you increase and practice greater resilience and thereby be more effective? What will it take? What will need to change and what will your implementation look like? Where will you bring forth courage to establish new priorities for yourself, your team, organization, and community? If you do, what will be gained? And, if you don't, what will be the cost?

CHAPTER
# 16

# Giving Up Carrying Other People's Lunch Boxes

*Before you are a leader, success is all about growing yourself. When you become a leader, success is all about growing others.*

– Jack Welch

Your employees understand their jobs. They know what they need to do to achieve their goals and meet expectations. If they don't, they are likely not the right people for the positions, or you have failed to give them the necessary tools to succeed. Once you are confident you have played your part in ensuring their success, it's time for you to let people do what they need to do—empower them to be accountable and make good decisions.

If you are committed to getting the most out of your employees—harnessing all of their talent, skill, and creativity—and help them gain the most fulfillment from their jobs, it's up to you to establish acceptance of responsibility. This includes responsibility for positive outcomes as well as for mistakes.

Giving employees the freedom to solve problems requires courage. You have to release control and possess the necessary confidence that they will choose the right path. Once you have set clear standards and communicated your expectations, it's time to delegate to them the freedom and responsibility to do their best work.

Each person on your team is a wellspring of potential. The degree to which you are able to tap into that will determine your success as a leader. If you expect, inspire, and encourage employees to perform at their highest levels, you foster learning and growth. Then, when you get out of the way, your success, and theirs, will improve. As Bill Hewlett, co-founder of Hewlett-Packard, says, "Men and women want to do a good job, and if they are provided with the proper environment, they will do so."

Companies that build a culture of empowerment have superior resilience. They usually surge ahead of their competitors and become leaders in their industry. San Diego Zoo Global, 3M, Southwest Airlines, Pizza Hut, and many other organizations are good examples. Employee empowerment has played an important role in these recognized brands. According to a study conducted by Pepperdine University, corporations that truly exhibit empowerment through emphasizing meaningful communication, willingness to serve, and common purpose will have statistically more favorable financial or investment results than those lacking employee empowerment.[1]

## The Lunch Box Story

When Sandy's son, Adam, was little, she carried his lunch box for him. Like any good mother or father, every day she would pack a healthy lunch and put it in his cubby when she dropped him off at pre-school. One day, his teacher, Tina, asked her why she carried Adam's lunch box. Exasperated, Sandy stated, "It's my job to take care of Adam's lunch."

The teacher responded, "Sandy, consider that Adam can carry his own lunch box."

After a few weeks and much introspection, Sandy came to realize that carrying Adam's lunch box was in fact a disservice. She was robbing him of the opportunity to be responsible and take owner-

[1] Stanley, Darrol J., DBA, "The Impact Of Empowered Employees On Corporate Value: The Corporate Culture Of The 100 Best Companies To Work For Offers The Key To Maximizing Shareholder Wealth," *Graziadio Business Review*, Pepperdine University, 2005 Volume 8 Issue 1

ship. So, Adam began to carry his own lunch box with great pride, and surprising ease, even though he was only three years old. Although this in itself wasn't a particularly significant event, it did establish a pattern of responsibility for him at an early age.

As often as she can remember, Sandy now asks herself "Where are there opportunities to encourage and inspire Adam to take owner-ship of his life?" Now a sophomore at UC Berkeley, he has grown into a self-sufficient, surprisingly independent, and very successful young man. Despite a demanding academic schedule, he does his own grocery shopping, cooks his own meals, does his laundry, and generally manages his wellbeing with finesse. He carries his own lunch box. Isn't this the dream of every parent, manager, or coach?

As she pondered the lunch box issue over the years, it became apparent to Sandy that this issue, at least metaphorically, is common in the corporate environment as well. As she has traveled the world inspiring others to create cultures of excellence in their organizations, she has found that it is common practice for leaders at all levels to carry employees' lunch boxes. They take more responsibility than wise or necessary by offering solutions, solving problems, and fixing break-downs rather than encouraging employees to find their own way.

Have you found yourself carrying other people's lunch boxes? Perhaps you might even have done the work for your team members on occasion? It is common for leaders to take responsibility for solving problems. Your title (and salary) implies that you are the "go to" person to make decisions and resolve issues. When people come to you with an issue, they typically have the expectation that you will take the "monkey off their back," so to speak. It can be tempting to help, but taking the monkey off their backs can often be nothing more than rescuing them. In so doing, you might cripple them by compromising their ability to respond appropriately next time. If you invest your time and energy to help them take the initiative and deal with the issue themselves, you develop their capacity, build their confidence, and condition them to take ownership in the future.

What if you gave up carrying other people's lunch boxes? What would happen if you allowed your team members to discover the solution, solve the problem, and learn while offering encouragement and support? Would it free you up to be more strategic and make wiser use of your energy to meet objectives?

## Doing the Right Things Without Being Told

The pathway to resilience is to give people the freedom to take initiative. People who have the freedom to solve problems, make improvements, deal with change, and provide exceptional customer service are more likely to weather storms and quickly bounce back from setbacks. Yet, in many cases employees may be reluctant to take the initiative they need to excel, in part because they feel their managers don't fully support them.

Managers who discourage risk taking and punish employees for failure often squelch employee initiative. "How a company deals with mistakes suggests how well it will wring the best ideas and talents out of its people, and how effectively it will respond to change," says Bill Gates, chairman and CEO of Microsoft Corporation. "When employees know that mistakes won't lead to retribution, it creates an atmosphere in which people are willing to take chances in order to come up with ideas and suggest changes. This environment is important to a company's long-term success."

## ROARING IDEAS

Zappos call-center employees are given the freedom to deliver a WOW experience for every customer. Employees can decide to refund a customer's money, upgrade shipping, make that customer a V.I.P., or send a surprise WOW package of cookies or flowers to brighten a customer's day.

## Raising Expectations Unleashes Potential

As John Quincy Adams once said, "If your actions inspire others to dream more, learn more, do more and become more, you are a leader." The more you expect of others, the greater the likelihood they will rise up to meet your expectations. On the other hand, if you don't expect much, people will not be inspired to contribute at a higher level.

People will inevitably work harder for something in which they feel they have ownership. A sense of ownership stems from involvement and participation in the organization beyond a person's particular job expectations. You can encourage ownership by playing to people's strengths, and acknowledging their efforts to help them build confidence in their abilities. Each time you reward ownership, it will reinforce the behavior and encourage repetition.

A recent SDZG initiative called the New Perspective group was composed of employees from all levels of the organization. It was established and inspired by president and CEO Doug Myers in an effort to invite voices from across the organization to participate in building and creating its vision. In Chapter 15, we referred to this initiative as a means to honor people's greatness. In addition to acknowledging hidden skills and talents, formation of the New Perspective group was a demonstration of confidence and commitment on the part of leaders to invite employees to participate at a higher level, and become more involved in SDZG's future.

"We realized that participants in this group may not have the necessary skill or experience to be part of high-level initiative like this," says Myers. "Nevertheless, we knew that this invitation communicated something far more important. It sent an important message to employees that we believe in them, that we want their voices to be heard, and that we are interested in them taking greater ownership in San Diego Zoo Global's success."

The New Perspective group was comprised of Millennials, Gen Y/Gen X'ers, and many newer to the organization—those who are "under the radar" in terms of leadership, yet identified by their managers as stars and possibly future leaders of the organization. They brought a fresh and new perspective to the strategic planning process, and have opened the eyes of the "more seasoned" employees who needed to see things differently. "This process was incredible for me; I was asked to weigh in on the future of the organization… and of ending extinction…when a few months prior it was doubtful if the executive team even knew who I was," remarked one New Perspective team member.

## ROARING IDEAS

Employee empowerment is a core value at Southwest Airlines. The company's leaders have limited formal structures and are trusting employees to make decisions. The result is a culture of positivity, and customers are the beneficiaries. This perspective has helped Southwest become the largest U.S. air carrier with the fewest customer complaints, and an example of operational efficiency.

## Building Self-Confidence and Focus

People believe they are empowered when they are left to their own devices to achieve results. It's worth the time and energy to allow them to act on their own decisions. By doing this, you help build confidence, allowing your team to become the experts, and hence the best. Leadership guru and best-selling author Marshall Goldsmith suggests there are several things an organization can do to build an environment that empowers people. One of these is not to second-guess people's decisions or shut down initiators. This undermines their confidence and heightens reluctance to take risk.

One of your most important roles as a leader is to build confidence in others. When people feel confident they're much more likely to take risks. Self-confident people are decisive, more focused, and more willing to learn and grow. These are your future leaders, the people who will help hold up your company in times of stress.

When self-confidence improves, so does productivity and morale. How can you build confidence? Point out where employees have taken risks and succeeded in the past. Ask them how they overcame an obstacle. Everyone has achieved something that demonstrates their strength and capability. "I make it a point to express confidence in my team's ability," says Dwight Scott, Zoo director. "I believe it's my primary role as a leader to reaffirm people's strengths, skills, and positive qualities. This helps to build their self-belief."

David Page, director of finance and SDZG controller, is a proponent of giving managers the tools they need to make good decisions. "In the past decade, we have built robust financial budgeting and reporting tools," explains Page. "These tools have allowed managers to track and manage their labor and expenses to a much greater degree." By empowering managers with the necessary resources, leaders now are able to "enforce budget compliance, a critical aspect of building financial responsibility and security for the future," according to Page.

## You Can't Do Everything on Your Own

You probably have way too much to do, buried in a never-ending list of tasks. Most leaders will agree that delegation is the most viable pathway to save time and help others develop new skills. Delegation is a critical skill. "Your most important task as a leader is to teach people how to think and ask the right questions so that the world doesn't go to hell if you take a day off," says Jeffrey Pfeffer, the Thomas D. Dee II professor of organizational behavior at Stanford University's Graduate School of Business and author of *What Were They Thinking?: Unconventional Wisdom About Management.* Yet, many leaders will overlook this opportunity.

There are many reasons leaders fail to delegate. A classic sign of inadequate delegation is overload. If you are working long hours and believe you're indispensable, that might be a sign you're not delegating frequently enough. Or, if you feel your team isn't taking over their share of projects, this could be a signal you're not tapping into their talents and skills. Of course, you want to be helpful and solve problems. That's your job. However, when you take on others' problems, you compromise your ability to get your work done. More importantly, you forego the necessary time to think strategically.

Delegating more means you have to be comfortable with letting the ball drop. This might sound contradictory to everything you believe about good leadership, but in the long term it's what is in the best interest of your company. Does it make sense to cover up for somebody by doing his or her job or hiding a problem? Or, does it serve everyone better in the long term, to allow the failure? Failure can provide a valuable opportunity for learning. It can be the seed of innovation and growth.

SDZG is taking this concept to heart, and a large part of its new Executive Leadership Development Program is devoted to delegating—in particular, what tasks are managers holding on to, that they will need to give up in order to move to the next level in their career. As a guiding force in this process, participants in this group are using some wisdom from Scott Elbin, as expressed in his book, *The Next*

*Level: What Insiders Know About Executive Success.* Elbin writes that "as you move to the next level, your passion needs to shift from a narrow focus to a broad focus. You could argue that making this shift is the essence of what it takes to make the shift from functional manager to executive leader." As part of the SDZG development program, participants are asked to designate what narrow functional task can be delegated away, allowing them to focus on more strategic issues.

If you're running ragged, you're exhausted, stressed, and burned out, it's time for you to examine your tasks and find ways to delegate. Lightening your workload begins with a willingness to stop carrying other people's lunch boxes. Do you have the discipline to refrain from your fixing and solving, and instead ask questions like, "What do you want to have happen?" "What do you see as the next step?" or "If this were all up to you, what do you believe is the best way forward?"

## Zoo Print for Success

* Assess the level of ownership in your organization.

* Identify ways in which you can create a more consistent culture of ownership.

* Develop a plan to inspire, encourage, and reward ownership.

## World-Famous Leadership Questions

* Whose lunch box are you carrying?

* What tasks and responsibilities can someone else on your team perform? Identify who has the skill and talent to take responsibility and then give it away.

* Develop a plan to delegate more.

## ROAR LOUDER

How can you build more self-confidence in your team so that people are more willing and able to generate fresh ideas, take risks, and show initiative?

CHAPTER
**17**

# Raising Leaders

*The final test of a leader is that he leaves behind him in
other men the conviction and the will to carry on.*

– Walter Lippmann

Winning a relay is often not about how fast you run, but how well
you pass the baton. The true measure of success for a leader is how he
or she raises leaders and plans for succession. Whether by plan or due
to some unexpected event, every leader's time of service will inevitably come to an end. San Diego Zoo Global is actively planning for
succession, building programs to raise the next generation of leaders
who will continue the world-famous legacy. SDZG leaders believe
that lasting leadership creates cohesive teams, compels cooperation,
retains valued employees, increases productivity, and boosts overall
pride in the organization.

## Leadership Development: Ensuring the Future

People respond with loyalty and dedication if you take a genuine
interest in their future. A well-developed leadership program builds
loyalty. Loyal employees are more engaged and more productive.
They are also more resilient. Today's savvy workers want to advance
and appreciate support in the process. Millennials, in particular, tend
to be ambitious and seek opportunities for quick career advancement. They want to be more versatile and add value to the organization. They want to gain skill. As one employee puts it, "My career

path at SDZG is to move into a management position and to do my part to help fulfill the organization's mission."

Leadership development programs don't have to be elaborate or costly. If the program is developed with sincere intention, and time and energy are focused on the right skills, the gains can be substantial. Despite the fact that the SDZG leadership development program is run on a very tight budget, it has significant impact.

SDZG president and CEO Doug Myers believes a robust leadership development program not only serves to develop individuals, but also helps to position SDZG as an industry leader. "We have changed our approach to employee development dramatically in the last decade," he says. "It's not that we didn't focus on our employees before. It's just that we hadn't tailored our training efforts to the kind of employee we want here."

Almost everybody in a professional position at SDZG has a bachelor's or advanced college degree. Employees at every level in the organization have access to continued education, on-the-job training, and opportunities to increase their knowledge as professionals.

SDZG has a standard practice of sending employees out to other zoos every year when it is financially viable. "I tell employees I don't want them looking for what the other zoo is doing wrong," Myers says. "I ask them to come back with an idea about what we can do better."

Myers and his team are passionate about creating an environment of learning and improvement. "We give our employees the opportunity to seek knowledge to be better at what they do," Myers explains. "Even if they choose to work somewhere else, they will take away skills and talent that will help them in their next professional opportunity." According to Myers, it is projected that within the next 10 years, of the 220 accredited zoos, 100 of their directors will retire. "If we excel at raising leaders, we'll have a lot of San Diego Zoo people managing zoos around the world," he says with pride.

## The Best Companies Foster Learning

Many organizations are in a constant state of upheaval, trying to do more with less. They invest more in the critical day-to-day tasks and neglect long-term activities, which often have a more significant payback. Sometimes leaders will say they don't have time for mentoring and developing their team. There is always time for what's important. If you believe that developing your people and growing leaders is critical to your organization's success, then you will find the time and resources.

The Best Companies for Leadership study, conducted by the Hay Group, surveys 17,000 individuals at 2,100 organizations in 115 countries. According to its 2014 survey, the best companies help leaders develop and rise within their organizations. Eighty percent of the top 20 companies have clear career paths for their employees, compared to only 48 percent of all other companies.

For fewer and fewer employees, a paycheck is their primary motivator at work. Most people in the workforce, especially the younger generation, thrive best and desire to work in an environment that fosters learning and growth. They also need to know there is opportunity for career advancement. This can include clear career paths, professional development, tuition reimbursement, ongoing learning opportunities, and mentorship programs.

The trend toward prioritizing development over compensation is reflected in studies such as one published by Glassdoor, which puts together a list of the top 25 companies offering the best career opportunities. This list is based on 432,000 company reviews by employees who voluntarily and anonymously share what their job and company is like. Topping the list are firms such as Bain & Company, Boston

Consulting Group, McKinsey & Company, Suncor, Four Seasons, and Schlumberger.

## Building Your Leadership Brand

As SDZG gains greater visibility and positive exposure with its best practices, there is a higher demand for excellence in leadership—at all levels. In an effort to align leaders to a common set of behaviors, SDZG developed the "world-famous" leadership branding statement to distinguish it in the marketplace. An effective brand is embodied in products, services, people, and guest experiences. Whereas the product or service brand reflects the customer's needs and stakeholder's aspirations, the leadership brand communicates the expectations people have of the way in which leaders behave.

### ZOOView

San Diego Zoo Global's Leadership Brand: We are fiercely committed to being ambassadors for wildlife, with unwavering focus on global collaboration and advocacy, innovation, development of our employees, and unrelenting passion for what we do.

SDZG's leadership brand is an expression of the commitment and passion leaders have to establishing a strong identity. It communicates who they are, what they want to be known for, and what they want others to say about them. It holds leaders at all levels accountable for the desired success behaviors.

The leadership brand is shared with all stakeholders as a means to solicit feedback and identify where leaders have opportunities to be more consistent. The tenets of the brand are taught, reviewed, and assessed in the Extraordinary Leadership training program.

According to HR experts Norm Smallwood and Dave Ulrich, a leadership brand is a reputation for developing outstanding managers who demonstrate a set of skills and talents that are tailored to fulfill the expectations of customers and stakeholders. Companies with a credible leadership brand inspire trust that they will keep promises and deliver on values. Smallwood and Ulrich teach that a leadership brand must be embedded into the company's culture, woven through its policies and reflected in expectations for employees.[1]

## Developing Extraordinary Leaders at SDZG

A cookie-cutter training program that offers generic off-the-shelf learning programs can fall short. Training that aligns with your company's vision, mission, and values, and is designed specifically to build employees' capacity to deliver on your promise will have greater benefit. SDZG's development programs are uniquely crafted and branded to address its need to build a world-famous team and deliver the ROAR—an exceptional guest experience.

SDZG leaders fiercely believe that strong leadership at all levels is the key to business success, and the best leaders are lifelong learners. "Everyone in our organization needs to be a lifelong learner," says Zoo Director Dwight Scott. He believes just as the vision sets the stage for where the organization wants to be in 10 to 20 years, so leaders ought to be looking into the future to determine how they will need to develop to fulfill their potential.

Leadership itself can be learned, as it is an observable pattern of practices and behaviors, and a definable set of skills and abilities. SDZG is committed to both individual and collective growth and development in the leadership journey, as well as to providing the tools needed for that success.

---

[1] Smallwood, Norm, and Ulrich, Dave, "Building a Leadership Brand," *Harvard Business Review,* July–August 2007

Yet, it's not so easy to provide world-class leadership training with a nonprofit budget. In 2004, there were no organizationally sponsored or internally created training programs at SDZG—not for customer service, not for skills training, and certainly not for leadership development. That changed in 2005 when SDZG created the umbrella moniker of "Zoo U" through the organizational strategic planning process. Since that time, a new program has been added every year, and now Zoo U offers several home-grown, grassroots leadership development programs.

The current "Zoo U" program is vast, and impressive—and it is administered on a shoestring budget of around $60,000 for 3,000 employees. This is done by use of internal knowledge (much training of trainers has occurred).

Leadership programs falling under the Zoo U umbrella include the Executive Leadership Development Program, the Extraordinary Leadership Training Program, and the Zoo U Exceptional Leaders Program.

## Executive Leadership Development Program

This year-long program prepares SDZG's current and future executives to translate leadership excellence into winning business results. The series is comprised of a blended-learning approach—participants not only receive executive coaching (both individual and in small cohorts), but meet five times throughout the year for in-person executive leadership training. In addition, all participants engage in a comprehensive 360 review process, with a corresponding annual development plan.

The SDZG Executive Leadership Development Program develops leaders who can:

❧ Drive performance in a changing world.

❧ Manage horizontal integration in a complex organization.

❧ Lead and develop talent.

❧ Make tough decisions.

It is built to help SDZG executives navigate a complex, often ambiguous role that requires them to:

❧ Embrace and support the long-range vision for the organization.

❧ Flourish in the face of new competitors from all corners of the globe.

❧ Be entrepreneurs who devise ways to innovatively meet client needs.

❧ Create a high-performance culture that elevates talent strategy to business strategy.

❧ Execute under intense scrutiny and with little leeway from their board, their business partners, the media, and the public at large.

## Extraordinary Leadership Training Program

This three-class series reinforces the core fundamentals of leadership. This includes incorporating SDZG's Rules of Engagement into the daily routine of leading people. The program is also a thorough review of core Z-Max Leadership Competencies, which all SDZG managers must live up to in order to be successful leaders within the organization, regardless of their departments, disciplines, or titles.

Topics covered include Passion, Engagement, and Innovation; The Rules of Engagement; 6 Core SDZG Leadership Competencies; and Mentoring, Collaboration, and Advocacy. These modules have been designed to provide pertinent information specifically branded to the SDZG leadership team, and to teach skills that will have an immediate, lasting impact.

## Exceptional Leaders Program

Another recent addition to the SDZG Zoo U oeuvre is the Exceptional Leaders Program, created to harness online learning as well as executive coaching. This program consists of a series of cutting-edge online leadership courses that participants have six months to complete. In addition, the groups meet regularly during the six months for a coaching and succession planning discussion, always led by two members of the SDZG Executive Team. Those gathered also reflect upon what was learned and share best practices.

As SDZG gains greater visibility and positive exposure with its best practices, there is a higher demand for excellence in leadership—at all levels. Beyond the well-crafted words, lasting leadership creates cohesive teams, compels cooperation, retains valued employees, increases productivity, and boosts overall pride in the organization.

SDZG continues to be recognized nationally for its training programs. There are currently several different iterations of leadership training, described in more detail below.

## San Diego Zoo Global Academy

The SDZG Academy is designed to harness the efficiencies of online learning to train internal staff as well as share SDZG's expertise around the world. An online learning portal, it offers a broad range of educational modules in an efficient, flexible, and cost-effective way. Academy learning titles span a wide range of subjects, from communication to animal care, as seen in Figure 17.1. "It has been a win-win solution for SDZG to leverage its intellectual property as well as serve organizations around the world," says Jon Prange, director of the SDZG Academy.

The SDZG Academy grew out of SDZG's animal training program. "Animal keeper training was outdated," says Bob Wiese, chief life sciences officer. "When I took this role, we began a concen-

# SDZG ACADEMY

**Animal Training**

- Zoonotic Disease
- Fundamentals in Animal Learning
- Regulations and Inspection Readiness
- Working Safely with Dangerous Animals
- Elephant Management
- Nutrition
- Record Keeping
- Behavior Management
- Life Support Systems
- Disaster Preparedness
- Enrichment
- Ethics
- Animal Handling and Restraint

**Webinars**

- Mapping Your Performance and Talent Strategy for Results
- Effective Onboarding— the San Diego Zoo Way!
- Roaring Rewards: Creating a World-Famous Employee Recognition Program
- Becoming a World-Famous Mentor
- Labor Law Roundup
- HR Strategic Planning
- Creating a World-Famous Culture in Your Workplace
- Creatively Implementing a 360 Program on a Budget
- Creating a World-Famous Employee Communications Strategy
- Hosting a World-Famous Summer Internship Program

*Figure 17.1 A partial list of San Diego Zoo Global Academy offerings*

trated effort to update the training, and investigate how we could use our resources to support other zoos."

Time and budget concerns made it difficult to take employees out of their jobs for two weeks to complete the training. "Even though the new training program was exemplary, we weren't able to get people through it," explains Wiese. "Even though keepers received good on-the-job training, they were falling behind in higher-level animal husbandry courses."

The advent of the online Academy made it possible for keepers to complete training requirements in short blocks of time, as job requirements allowed. "Now, we are able to get all new staff trained quickly and easily," Wiese reports. "Smaller zoos benefit from the expertise of the SDZG animal staff that they would never have at their own institutions," Wiese says. The Academy is an excellent source of non-gate revenue, and at the same time serves the greater good. "The bottom line is keepers both at SDZG and zoos around the world are now better trained," Wiese concludes.

## Roar Louder

These popular monthly manager forums, aimed at creating stronger leaders, are offered monthly at both campuses. They cover everything from new SDZG programs to leadership/management skills, wellness, and labor and employment law classes. The instructors are a combination of in-house leaders, or external consultants who support the Zoo either via a highly reduced fee or through trade of zoo tickets.

Managers are required to attend at least six sessions annually, but of the 300-plus members of the SDZG manager team, over 75 percent attend at least 10 each year. SDZG managers are polled on the topics for which they would like more training, and this helps to form the schedule of Roar Louder forums for the following year.

Managers who meet their "quota" of Roar Louder workshops are rewarded at the annual manager holiday party with a special gift. These can be a watch, personalized binders, jackets, and other highly desirable items.

## Roar Stronger

These quarterly forums for all non-managerial employees are designed to empower them to become more well-rounded and motivated. They are optional, but those who complete at least two of the four sessions are rewarded with vacation hours.

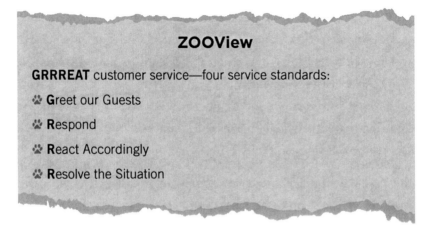

**ZOOView**

**GRRREAT** customer service—four service standards:

🐾 **G**reet our Guests

🐾 **R**espond

🐾 **R**eact Accordingly

🐾 **R**esolve the Situation

## Nurturing Future Leaders

Zoo U's "Passport to the Future" college relations program is a key component of SDZG's strategic plan. The college program supplements the Zoo's and Safari Park's summer staffing strategy by inviting college students in related disciplines to receive valuable experience and specialized training. College interns fill roles as Skyfari aerial tramway operators, education camp counselors, merchandising sales clerks, and other positions. They are also assigned business projects to ensure that they gain an understanding of the business aspects of the organization

From a very young age, Jamie had a passion for animals and a desire to learn more about them. "My family and I were members of the Zoo and visited often," she explains. "When I was accepted into San Diego State University (SDSU), it seemed only natural to study zoology."

With a love for educating people about animals, Jamie knew that her future was at the Zoo. "I began by volunteering at Lions, Tigers & Bears Big Cat & Exotic Animal Rescue, where I experienced first-hand how hard work and dedication to the care and wellbeing of animals can inspire people," Jamie says.

With a desire to make her dream of working at the Zoo a reality, Jamie interviewed as many keepers as possible to find out what it would take to land her dream job. "They said to have a passion to save species for future generations, be ready to work weekends and holidays, in any weather and at any time, but with the assurance of knowing that what you do makes a difference."

Jamie got her foot in the door with an offer of an internship at the Zoo the summer after her junior year of college. As an intern working at the Skyfari aerial tramway, she was able to sit in on supervisor meetings and learn some of the ins and outs of the Zoo. "Although I was not yet working with the animals, I felt like I was a part of the mission to educate the public about our vision." After her internship, Jamie was offered a part-time position at Skyfari. "I was finally a real employee of the Zoo and one step closer to being a keeper," she excitedly explains.

A year later, after graduating from SDSU, Jamie was selected for a "loan" in the Children's Zoo. "I was working behind the scenes, caring for the animals, and on stage talking to the guests. I had a taste of my dream, but I wasn't there yet," she remembers.

Another year passed and Jamie finally was offered a part-time keeper position. "Every day I worked with the other keepers, but I didn't have the khakis with my name on it. I wasn't official. Bouncing back and forth between departments, I had a unique chance to see every side of what makes this Zoo great, and I wouldn't trade that experience for the world."

Not long after Jamie was offered a full-time keeper position at the Children's Zoo. "I finally made it," she enthuses. "Prayer, patience, and perseverance paid off. I am a full-time keeper at the San Diego Zoo, my dream has come true, and it is better than I could have ever imagined."

## ZOOView

Education and outreach form the essential cornerstones of any successful conservation endeavor. So in addition to developing internal leaders, SDZG cultivates a community of future conservationists through Science, Technology, Engineering, and Math (STEM) education programs. Focusing on high school and college students, SDZG's classroom, field, and online programs use STEM to foster curiosity-driven bonds and empathy with the natural world. SDZG's educational branch houses multiple classrooms, which provide access to innovative technology, groundbreaking research, and once-in-a-lifetime encounters. Students leave with an understanding of STEM-related careers, and college trajectories based on interaction with devoted academic and industry mentors.

## Cultivating Potential through Mentoring

Every employee who has potential deserves to be cultivated. Mentoring programs are an effective strategy to give personal attention and guidance to nurture and develop your most valuable employees. By connecting your high-potential team members with top performers in your company and others, it gives them access to personalized guidance and coaching to help them create readiness for leadership positions. Nowadays, anybody who is successful will tell you they've had a mentor who helped them socialize and understand how to navigate the corporate world. Mentoring has become part of our culture. Employees expect it.

As part of the College Relations Program, each intern is assigned a mentor who is also an SDZG manager. Each mentor goes through a San Diego Zoo Global Zoo U Mentor Training Program. The Purpose Statement of the SDZG Mentor Program is "To facilitate the professional development of the protégé through effective mentoring so that their experience at San Diego Zoo Global is 'World-Famous'."

And with that, SDZG has raving fans applying discretionary time to the organization's best interests and a booming morale from high levels of engagement—allowing for greater operating revenue for its mission.

The key tenets of this program are the various roles of mentors at SDZG—for example, teacher, sponsor, counselor, guide, buddy, and role model. According to Amy Adams, HR manager and trainer of the mentor program, "A world-famous mentor is responsive, a good listener, understanding, and compassionate, non-judgmental and ethical, approachable, and available, and has genuine interest in the development of the protégé."

## ROARING IDEAS

A 2013 Vestrics study examined responses from more than 830 mentees and 670 mentors participating in Sun Microsystem's program. Employee retention rates climbed 69 percent for the mentors and 72 percent for the mentees over the seven-year period of the study. The increased retention resulted in a savings of $6.7 billion in avoided staff turnover and replacement costs.

## Planning for the Future

If your CEO dies suddenly, who will take his or her place? What would you do if one of your most valuable executives is wooed away to a competitor? Do you have the next generation of leaders lined up to fill the most important roles in your organization? Do you have a plan in place to replace important people when they retire?

"Every company has a succession planning document," says David Larcker, a professor in the graduate school of business at Stanford University. "The question you have to ask is, 'Will it be operational?'"

SDZG has created a robust succession planning program that aligns the performance management process with the vision to "end extinction." It ensures employees at every level have ample opportunities to develop their leadership skills and guarantee that there is a leadership plan in place.

## Zoo Print for Success

🐾 Assess the effectiveness of your organization's leadership development program. Does it effectively build the necessary capabilities to fulfill your vision?

🐾 Identify any gaps where employees would benefit from more training and mentoring.

🐾 Develop a plan to ensure your organization's future leadership is in place.

## World-Famous Leadership Questions

🐾 Which next-level leadership skills are you committed to mastering?

🐾 Who will benefit from your personal guidance and attention through a mentoring relationship?

🐾 If you were to suddenly take ill or die, who would replace you?

## ROAR LOUDER

If, in five years, you want to be better than you are today; and, in ten years, you want to be better than you'll be in five years, what would you be doing differently now?

CHAPTER

# 18

# Shaking Things Up

*The tragedy of life is often not in our failure, but rather*
*in our complacency; not in our doing too much, but rather*
*in our doing too little; not in our living above our ability,*
*but rather in our living below our capacities.*

– Benjamin E. Mays

Change is constant. It is the nature of the workplace. Whether it's developing new products, launching new services, merging, downsizing, or exploring new strategies, dealing with change is inevitable. When embraced, change creates new possibilities. It opens the doors to growth and unanticipated gains.

Often change is uncomfortable, but you can revel in discomfort and use it to fuel your growth. Success is a result of stretching outside your comfort zone to the unknown, unproven, and unchartered. It requires an unwillingness to settle for the way things are, and to constantly challenge others and yourself.

Since the days of founder Dr. Harry Wegeforth, San Diego Zoo Global has been known for embracing change—dedicating itself to discovering fresh opportunities, better ways to work, and fruitful ways to innovate. One day, SDZG President and CEO Doug Myers was walking around the Safari Park with its founder, Dr. Charles Schroeder, discussing some changes he wanted to make. "The ideas I pitched to Dr. Schroeder were very different than the way in which we had approached our business in the past," says Myers. "But, I knew the bottom line is to make the bottom line."

Dr. Schroeder responded to Myers with the adage, "Your job is to respect the past and change the future."

"Schroeder never told me what to do, but he always gave me the freedom to think outside the box," Myers continues. Respecting the past is "remembering the roar" —that of the lion Dr. Harry heard in 1916—and to pass that roar along. "We should never forget where we came from and, at the same time, never stop innovating," says Myers.

## Inspiring Vision

The success of any change comes down to your ability as a leader to inspire the vision—to get people excited about the future, and engage them in being part of the transformation. When change is framed as an opportunity to create a new possibility, it leads to an exciting outcome. People become less resistant, less fearful of the uncertainty. The key to effective change is to clearly express the potential payoff or reward for each individual. How will they win?

Like the leopard, most people don't "change their spots," but prefer to stay within their comfort zone and avoid unnecessary change. What holds them back? Mindset.

Old patterns and ways of thinking can keep you stuck in status quo. A commitment to the way it used to be, how you used to do it, and how it has worked in the past restricts your capability to innovate. In order to change and grow, it is imperative to challenge old assumptions, every one of them. Rethinking the way you do things keeps your organization agile and relevant. The challenge is to avoid complexity. Keep change simple to avoid change fatigue.

Futurist and innovation expert Lisa Bodell recognizes the consequences of static and uninspired business practices. In her book,

*Kill the Company: End the Status Quo, Start an Innovation Revolution*, Bodell speaks to breaking down worn-out norms and adopting new behaviors to simplify the work experience. She suggests the very structures that were put in place to help companies grow are now holding them back. The result is complacency, with little or no change. She urges companies to create a culture of curiosity, to reawaken the ability to think, innovate, and grow.[1]

## ROARING IDEAS

Established in 2010, eyewear purveyor Warby Parker demonstrated how to challenge the status quo and abandon traditional ways of doing business when it transformed a medical necessity into a fashion accessory. It cut out the middleman to offer low prices, adding a hip factor, and a socially conscious approach to offer trendy eyeglasses for half of what other retailers charge.

## Challenging the Status Quo

The question in any company isn't are you good at what you do, but rather are you good enough to get better. As Jim Collins, author of *Good to Great*, says, "Good is the enemy of great." According to Collins, good is the main reason why things don't become great. Most companies don't become great, because they are good. It's easy to settle for good. Good breeds complacency. It creates a comfort zone that shuts down radical thinking and crushes creativity.

True leaders must constantly challenge the organization's boundaries, stretching employees to reinvent themselves. "One of the first things that I did when I took the role as zoo director, is to meet

[1] Bodell, Lisa, *Kill the Company: End the Status Quo, Start an Innovation Revolution*, Bibliomotion 2012

with my direct report group to communicate expectations," explains Dwight Scott. "Then I asked them to share their expectations of me." Scott's upfront expectation was for every person to commit to being a lifelong learner, to constantly challenge the status quo. "Whether they've been with the organization for 5 years or 45 years, I need every person on my team to see things like new, and to relentlessly question the way things are."

You do this to fulfill your organization's potential and to serve the greater good. Protected contact with elephants is an example of how SDZG chartered new territory, challenged old paradigms, and spearheaded a radical change in animal care globally.

"Back in the day, people taking care of elephants would go into the enclosure with them," says Becky Lynn, director of employee communications. "Keepers would wash down the elephants and open their mouths so their tusks could be checked." Those keepers would pet and scratch the elephants. Then one day, a SDZG keeper was killed when one elephant moved too quickly. Myers and his team were devastated by the incident. They decided a change was necessary. It was time to rethink the basic assumptions of elephant care and create a new process that would protect people's safety and continue to provide quality care for the elephants.

"The keeper was very experienced with elephants, but you can't predict what a wild animal is going to do," Lynn explains. The zoo community was rife with stories of similar incidents. At one point, being an elephant keeper was considered the most dangerous job you could have.

Myers then decided that these specialists were no longer going to enter the elephant enclosure. "We're going to take care of them with a barrier between us," he declared.

At first, naysayers said it couldn't be done. Animal behaviorists insisted that it was necessary for keepers to enter the enclosures, to make contact, and if necessary, use negative reinforcement to manage their behavior. Myers insisted that he was not willing to lose another keeper. "I knew there had to be a way to tend to these animals without jeopardizing the safety of animal care employees," he says.

There was. "We were able to train the elephants in these new behaviors with positive reinforcement and special training techniques," explains Gary Priest, curator of animal behavior. (One by one, other zoos around the world followed SDZG's lead. The protocol is now called "protected contact.")

Myers took a controversial stand, changing not only how SDZG worked with elephants but also working to get all accredited zoos to make the change. "I spoke to other zoo directors, sharing the tragedy that happened at our park and the success we had creating a new way of working with elephants," he explains. "Once we had created an alternative system, directors had a choice and no one wants to be the director responsible for someone's death,"

"Myers led the charge in a highly contentious environment," notes Beth Branning, corporate director of vision, innovation, and strategy. "I was at the meeting where the decision was made. I watched as each member aligned with Doug. It was a matter of if the San Diego Zoo is doing it this way, then we ought to as well. Doug's courage to challenge the zoological community had significant impact on the safety of keepers and guests."

## ZOOView

Trike around a zoo? Who would have thought! Now you can explore the African Plains and the Asian Savanna at the San Diego Zoo Safari Park on a custom-made, motorized trike. Guides provide insights into the animals roaming the Asian field habitats, as well as conservation work around the world. The tour includes photo stops and unique visual opportunities in Safari Park areas not accessible on foot.

## Testing Grace and Steadfastness

San Diego Zoo Global leaders are courageous in their commitment to being "world famous." They face many obstacles that test their grace and steadfastness, and yet continue to insist on excellence. Courage is every leader's most valuable asset. When people observe the lion in nature, they detect an easy strength and courage coupled with a natural dignity. The lion is born powerful, and that power comes naturally to it. The lion has no need for false bravado.

Leaders at SDZG encourage employees to exhibit courage and be fearless. "One of my lawyers told me that our employees are the most politically proper and tenacious people he's ever met," Myers says. "We're known as relentless. We just do not give up. When we see something and we believe it's the right thing, we want to do it right and we do whatever it takes to make the necessary change."

When Tim joined SDZG in 2004, he boldly declared to Myers and the search committee that in one year the organization was going to be recognized as an employer of choice and win awards for being a stellar place to work. This was a lofty statement, since in its 88 years in existence, SDZG had not been heralded in that way. But the HR team, energized by the challenge, strategically started to change things. In time, they managed to establish a reputation around San Diego, the zoo industry, and the HR landscape nationwide that major changes were in the works. People began to take a look at the great programs SDZG was putting in place for its employees.

Yes, the Zoo had amazing animals, but the focus started to shift to how well the employees were treated, how engaged they were, and what unique programs were in place—all on a non-profit budget. In the fall of 2005, SDZG was named the Best Place to Work in San Diego by the Society for Human Resource Management (SHRM). This was due, in part, to the tenacity of the HR team striving for that goal, and going after an end result that had not been thought possible in the past.

## ROARING IDEAS

Another example of changing things up—in this case, altering the paradigm for retail, came from Five Below, which combined dollar-store prices with a teen-friendly vibe. The rapidly expanding retailer caters to the wants of young customers on a treasure hunt for the latest, greatest gadgets.

## Embracing and Activating Stakeholders

SDZG is currently navigating one of the biggest risks it has ever taken. It is changing its identity from a zoo with a very high-quality conservation research department, to a conservation organization that happens to run two really great zoos. "These are very different identities," explains Dr. Allison Alberts, chief conservation and research officer. "One of the biggest challenges SDZG faces is how to make employees feel like they are part of it. We don't want anyone to feel they're being left behind. If someone is working in retail, we have to answer the question of how that person's skills and talents apply to conservation."

Gaining employee support for the identity change is key to SDZG's success. Equally as important is the risk of losing public support. "If people have always thought of San Diego Zoo as a fantastic zoo, you don't want them to suddenly think that you're no longer a zoo," says Dr. Alberts. "You want them still to think that you're a great zoo, but you want them to understand that you're so much more than a zoo." The challenge for SDZG is to engage internal and external stakeholders in understanding the value of being known as a conservation organization rather than just a "world-famous" zoo. "We want people to embrace the fact that we are working in 80 countries around the world, that we are committed to species survival, and not just taking great care of the animals at the zoo," Alberts explains.

"Strengthening our conservation identity can be a challenge," agrees Chief Marketing Officer Ted Molter. SDZG's initial vision was connecting people to wildlife and conservation. "We felt like we got there in three years."

SDZG's larger mission of ending extinction won't be achieved in the short-term, and leaders at all levels will be challenged to keep the momentum going. "The challenge will be to engage people in it for the long haul," explains Alberts. "We realize the issue of extinction won't be completely resolved. We know some species are going to go extinct. Nevertheless we must dedicate ourselves to this cause. We just need to put our necks out there."

## ZOOView

The early bird gets the worm. Arrive at the San Diego Zoo early to have breakfast with pandas Xiao Liwu, Bai Yun, and/or Gao Gao while you get the latest info on the popular bamboo bears! The Early Morning with Pandas is a two-hour adventure that also includes a tour around the Zoo in a shuttle cart, with stops to visit some of our other animals up close—just another example of how SDZG has created opportunity by shaking things up.

## Shaking Up Routines

Just like in other organizations, SDZG could easily settle into its ways and become resigned and cynical. Cynicism and resignation breed repetitive behaviors, a throwing up of hands in hopelessness and helplessness. But, one play can change everything. When one person has the courage to press through and chart a new course—to spark a new possibility—everything changes. Sometimes you have to pierce the pattern, shake up routines, and see things differently.

As a leader, it is your imperative to periodically wake up your organization to establish a new viewpoint. You must pierce through existing patterns, disrupt the way things have always been done, and build new awareness. Just as you adjust the thermostat in your building to regulate the temperature, so must you adjust the natural set point of your team—the level of engagement or performance that had become the norm. Over time, people settle into a way of being, standards slip, and stagnancy creeps in. It requires a conscious decision as a leader to change the setting and expect a new quality of thinking and doing.

For all the businesses that have become obsolete due to changing consumer preferences, there are others that are capitalizing on changing trends, and using them to catapult their expansion. These disruptors are changing the way in which industries attract consumers.

For example, at the San Diego Zoo Safari Park, the traditional guest experience has been shaken up by the introduction of "the safari concept" as part of its rebranding from being called the "Wild Animal Park." This endeavor engendered much local discussion.

This portion of the experience is no longer the traditional single admission ticket, as with most zoos and attractions. Instead, you choose what type of "safari" on which you want to embark, with choices being the standard African Tram Safari, or such "premium product" upgrades as the Flightline Safari zipline, the Ropes Course Safari, special "cart" tour safaris, a "Roar and Snore" sleepover safari, or a Trike Safari.

The results have been phenomenal. Not only has attendance and revenue spiked, but the Safari Park has firmly established itself as a unique zoo experience, focused more on adventure and seeing animals roaming in large Africa-like savannas.

## Zoo Print for Success

- Assess how well your company has developed acceptance and appreciation of change.

- Identify how effectively you encourage employees to exhibit courage and be fearless.

- Develop a plan to shake things up, to disrupt traditional models to spark more innovation and creativity.

## World-Famous Leadership Questions

- How does your team respond to change?

- What is your team's current set point? What are the accepted levels of performance?

- When last did you shake things up to stimulate a new level of creativity and innovation?

## ROAR LOUDER

If you had the courage to get outside your comfort zone, what new possibilities would you create for yourself and your team?

CHAPTER
**19**

# Creating Great Leadership with Courage

*Courage doesn't always roar. Sometimes courage is the quiet voice at the*
*end of the day saying, "I will try again tomorrow."*

– Mary Anne Radmacher

Leadership is an honor and a privilege. With that comes responsibility—to relentlessly challenge your boundaries, stretch, and grow, to always be seeking the next level of leadership mastery. Leadership conveys a duty to realize your fullest potential and the potential of others.

We live in a world that is constantly evolving. Most likely, you work in an environment that is advancing rapidly. To keep up, you have to be evolving. You are either in growth or decay. There is no middle ground. As Ray Kroc, founder of McDonald's Corporation, once said, "When you're green, you grow. When you're ripe, you rot."

## Confronting Your Growing Edge

How voracious an appetite do you have to confront your growing edge—where you bump up against resistance, feel uncomfortable, experience frustration, pain, or failure?

Your growing edge is the area in which you want to achieve greater success, and, more importantly, more lasting fulfillment. To find your growing edge, you need only look out into your work world and ask yourself: "What would I like to see happen? Where would I like to go? What would help me and my team get ahead and serve the greater good?"

When you challenge your edges, you reach deeper, see farther, and unlock added ingenuity. Tiny steps may not get you very far. Sometimes you must choose a leap sideways and beyond. This begins with your willingness to make unreasonable requests of yourself. World-famous leaders make it a point to keep stirring things up, alter routines, and break old habits. You push past current routines by zeroing in on the edge of them. You consider how you can build on them, reinvent them, or skip them altogether.

To continue evolving as a leader, you must say "no" to the drug of gradualness. Martin Luther King Jr., spoke out against making slow changes. Either we risk or we don't, he said. Either we change or we don't. The middle ground lulls you into complacency. Lasting change comes when you leap. Do you have the guts to keep challenging yourself?

## ROARING IDEAS

A lion or tiger can roar as loud as 114 decibels, about 25 times louder than a gas-powered lawn mower.[1] When the lion roars, it is communicating its supremacy to the Animal Kingdom. Now that's resilience, and analogous to the organizational roar that you can invoke through courageous leadership!

## Roar into Courageous Leadership

When the lion roars, all other animals are silenced. They don't dare make a sound in response, let alone come out into the open to face the fearless lion. The lion, the embodiment of power and unsurpassable strength, is a symbol of might, speed, and courage.

---

[1] Zielinski, Sarah, "Secrets of a Lion's Roar," Smithsonian.com, November 3, 2011

Courageous leadership necessitates you taking action that would typically stop you. It invites you to pierce through fear, worry, or doubt. A courageous leader stands in certainty and exudes self-confidence rather than arrogance, strength rather than control. These are times that require bold, confident, courageous leadership. Leaders who have the guts to take risks and break through barriers will be those who are most respected.

Demonstrating leadership courage can be uncomfortable. Whether it's having a tough conversation, making a contested decision, or accepting criticism, it is based in humility and a never-ending desire to learn and grow. Courageous leaders chart new frontiers and face adversity head-on. You put your most prized assets, your people, before profits. You are willing to be authentic, vulnerable, and transparent. You are continually growing and learning, always challenging the status quo, striving to reach the next level of mastery, and taking a vigilant stand for every person in the organization to realize more of his or her potential.

As a courageous leader, you listen, invite candid feedback, and say what needs to be said. You give other people the credit and hold yourself to the highest levels of accountability. You have the honesty to admit when you've made a mistake. You don't let your pride lead you in the wrong direction. You own up to errors and make things right. You are willing to embrace new ideas and challenge old assumptions.

> *"What makes a king out of a slave? Courage! What makes the flag on the mast to wave? Courage!"*
> – The Cowardly Lion in *The Wizard of Oz*

## Establishing a Unique Footprint

To maintain a world-famous organization, SDZG depends on courageous leaders. The SDZG brand, its reputation and identity, is shaped by the way in which its leaders lead, how they are known. "Our leadership reputation, individually and collectively as a leadership team, is either strengthening or weakening our identity," says Doug Myers, SDZG president and CEO. "To establish a compelling leadership brand, we must constantly challenge the organization's boundaries, and reinvent ourselves."

The leadership team at SDZG lives and breathes their vision with every action, every decision. Their genuine intention is to establish a unique footprint. "We ought to always be thinking about our legacy. It's our duty and responsibility and others want us to reveal it," says Ted Molter, chief marketing officer. "We strive to ensure that our legacy authentically represents who we are, and what we stand for."

SDZG's leadership legacy answers the question: how do we want to be remembered? What do we want others to say about us when we're listening and, more importantly, when we aren't? Myers and his leadership team are relentlessly focused on what they will leave behind that will continue be an inspiration for others. Will their legacy account for the needs of others and the advancement of conservation? They realize their legacy will not only be the way in which they are remembered, but also how the San Diego Zoo, Safari Park, and Institute for Conservation Research are remembered. This legacy, like the "roar," will be heard all around, near and far, and it will outlive them.

SDZG's leaders, comprised of nearly 300 supervisors, managers, directors, curators, and executive team members, have proven themselves as resilient, and world-famous, in their 100 years of success. As they entered their centennial-year celebration in 2016, their leadership brand became ever more important. They must live and breathe it. They must embody its mantra of representing world-famous ambassadors for wildlife, having unwavering focus on global collaboration and advocacy, staying relevant and innovative—all while keeping a 100-percent focus on employee engagement and development, with an unrelenting passion for what they do. It shows.

## Lean into Your Growing Edge

Like the butterfly, you begin your leadership journey as a caterpillar, absorbing as much knowledge as possible, engaging in continual learning and improvement, reading and seeking nourishment to help you grow. As you shed old paradigms and belief systems, you recreate yourself as you search for your truth and find your way. At some point, you shrug off the old in search of freedom—freedom from the past, old constructs, structures, and processes.

The shedding isn't always an easy process, as you battle with your ego, the establishment, or the way things have always been done. It can be painful. The emergence of the butterfly is resonant with the evolution and the realization of your potential, the promise of new life. Like the caterpillar, you must be patient as you surrender yourself to the process of transformation and the emergence of a more brilliant version of yourself.

Transformation begins with awareness of where you are currently, and inventorying what you already have to service this vision. Once you have identified the gap between where you are and where you want to be, then you ask, "Who will I need to be to get from here to there?" This is where you dive into willingness, yielding, and allowing yourself to transform. You stand in the field of becoming with radical honesty and you let go of what no longer services you. In reaching forward and achieving the next level of success, you inevitably have to become someone different.

## Zoo Print for Success

❧ Define what legacy your organization wishes to leave.

❧ Determine what leadership characteristics, attributes, and skill-set your leadership team will need to develop to fulfill this legacy.

❧ Identify ways in which you can deliberately and consciously build your legacy on a day-to-day basis.

## World-Famous Leadership Questions

❧ What new mindset, skill-sets, or tools do you want to refine and sharpen to become the best version of yourself? What is your growing edge?

❧ What fears, doubts, or worries do you need to overcome to lead to more courage?

❧ What is your unique leadership footprint?

## ROAR LOUDER

What will your leadership legacy be? How do you want to be remembered after you have gone? What would you need to do differently beginning today to create this legacy?

> *I am here for a purpose and that purpose is to grow into a mountain, not to shrink to a grain of sand. Henceforth will I apply all my efforts to become the highest mountain of all and I will strain my potential until it cries for mercy.*
>
> – Og Mandino

# SDZG HR Programs

## Z-Cares

Our suite of Human Resources-developed benefits programs including Z-Tirement, Zoo Perks, HealthLynx, and Roar Longer.

| | |
|---|---|
| **Z-Tirement** | 403(b), Pension, Financial Advice, Retirement Education, Retirement Benefits, and Retirement Oversight Committee |
| **Zoo Perks** | On-site offers, guest passes, local business discounts, local service discounts, financial perks, and local attraction discounts for employees |
| **Health Lynx** | Subsidized health benefits, Employee Assistance Program, and Paid Sick Leave |
| **Roar Longer Wellness Program** | Wellness Portal, Incentives, Health Risk Assessment, Biometric Screening, medical leaves, Zero Time-Loss Program, financial wellness incentives, and wellness education |

## Communication

Produced and maintained internally, our unique organization calls for unique and engaging methods of employee communication.

| | |
|---|---|
| **Roar Back! Employee Satisfaction and Engagement Survey** | Launched during employee appreciation month, this organizational strategic plan initiative usually garners close to 100% voluntary participation. The Roar Back Survey is meant to give managers honest and helpful feedback from employees and ensure organizational focus on engagement. |

| | |
|---|---|
| **Rules of Engagement** | Based on the Excellence Principles, these seven unique rules provide us with an engaging and uniform code of conduct standardized and practiced throughout our world-famous organization. |
| **Z-Max** | Online performance management program, which includes performance feedback, goals, development plans, and online training classes. |
| **ZOOView** | Monthly employee publication highlighting our conservation and animal care activities, as well as employee accomplishments and recognition, Rules of Engagement (code of conduct), and GRRREAT Customer Service. |
| **GRRREAT News** | Internal publication sharing organizational achievements and positive feedback both internally and from guests. |

## Zoo U

Programs and courses aimed at empowering our employees to become more a well-rounded, well-versed, and engaged staff within our organization both at work and at home.

| | |
|---|---|
| **Roar Stronger** | Quarterly forums for all nonmanagerial employees aimed at empowering them to become more well-rounded, well-versed, and motivated within our organization. |
| **Roar Louder** | This series of monthly manager forums is aimed at creating better, stronger leaders within our organization. |
| **Zoo U College Relations Program** | Bringing in college students who want to make a career of this industry, we give them assignments ensuring they gain a real understanding of key business drivers. |

| | |
|---|---|
| **Zoo U Leadership Training Programs** | Current programs include: Executive Leadership Development Program, Extraordinary Leadership Training Program, and the Exceptional Leaders Program. |
| **GRRREAT Customer Service Training Program** | Mandatory class for all employees to train in the basics of offering outstanding guest service to our guests, members, and each other. |
| **Roar Corps** | This program was designed to help foster development of future animal care staff, which can/will lead to permanent opportunities within these departments. |
| **San Diego Zoo Global Academy** | A powerful online learning platform that harnesses the expertise of San Diego Zoo Global and its partners to offer courses that meet the specific needs of individuals in the zoological profession. |
| **Learning Lab** | Designated areas at both campuses promoting online educational training via open-access computers and extended hours for employees. |

## Roaring Rewards

San Diego Zoo Global's suite of reward and recognition programs

| | |
|---|---|
| **Zooper Troopers** | Acknowledgment and incentive program for employees reaching 5, 10, 15, 20, etc. years of consecutive service. |
| **Zooper Heroes** | Nominated by management peers, this program acknowledges and rewards supervisors and managers for a single outstanding act or consistent behavior utilizing SDZG core values. |
| **Zooper Stars** | Nominated by management, this program acknowledges and rewards non-supervisory employees for a single, outstanding act or consistent behavior utilizing SDZG core values. |

| Zooper Bowl | Quarterly gathering to recognize and reward Zooper Stars and Zooper Troopers. |
| --- | --- |
| Zoo 20 Club | Annual dinner at the Zoo to reward and recognize employees and former employees who have reached 20+ years of consecutive service. |
| Zooper Market | Online merchandise listing and purchasing tool for departments to obtain incentives with an annual allotment of funds based on the number of employees in each area. |
| Visit-A-Job | Employees participate in the program after one year of service. On the month of their birthday, names are drawn, and winners choose a job within the organization to shadow for a day. |
| Z-Tech | Special perk whereby employees can purchase discount computer/electronic equipment for personal use and pay via payroll deduction. |

# INDEX

Note: Page numbers with
    *f* represent figures.

# Credits

*Publisher/Editorial Director: Michael Roney*

*Art Director: Sarah M. Clarehart*

*Copyeditor/Proofreader: Dan Cafaro*

*Indexer: Karl Ackley*

*Contact: info@highpointpubs.com*

**HIGHPOINT EXECUTIVE PUBLISHING**

**www.highpointpubs.com**